Landing a Library Job

Landing a Library Job

Deloris Jackson Foxworth

ROWMAN & LITTLEFIELD
Lanham • Boulder • New York • London

Published by Rowman & Littlefield
An imprint of The Rowman & Littlefield Publishing Group, Inc.
4501 Forbes Boulevard, Suite 200, Lanham, Maryland 20706
www.rowman.com

6 Tinworth Street, London, SE11 5AL, United Kingdom

Copyright © 2019 by The Rowman & Littlefield Publishing Group, Inc.

All rights reserved. No part of this book may be reproduced in any form or by any electronic or mechanical means, including information storage and retrieval systems, without written permission from the publisher, except by a reviewer who may quote passages in a review.

British Library Cataloguing in Publication Information Available

Library of Congress Cataloging-in-Publication Data

Names: Foxworth, Deloris Jackson, 1977– author.
Title: Landing a library job / Deloris Jackson Foxworth.
Description: Lanham : Rowman & Littlefield, [2019] | Includes bibliographical references and index.
Identifiers: LCCN 2018056379 (print) | LCCN 2018058009 (ebook) | ISBN 9781538117002 (Electronic) | ISBN 9781538116999 (pbk. : alk. paper)
Subjects: LCSH: Library science—Vocational guidance—United States.
Classification: LCC Z682.35.V62 (ebook) | LCC Z682.35.V62 F69 2019 (print) | DC 020.23—dc23
LC record available at https://lccn.loc.gov/2018056379

∞™ The paper used in this publication meets the minimum requirements of American National Standard for Information Sciences—Permanence of Paper for Printed Library Materials, ANSI/NISO Z39.48-1992.

Printed in the United States of America

To my mom, Pat, and my twin sister, Dorislee.

And an extra-special thanks to
Chris, Shelby, and Ashlee.
I love you with all my heart.

Contents

List of Figures	ix
List of Tables	xi
Preface	xiii
1 Identifying Types of Jobs	1
2 Finding Jobs	23
3 Applying for Jobs	49
4 Interviewing for Jobs	85
5 Following the Interview	117
6 Staying Relevant	141
Appendix 1 Professional Associations	169
Appendix 2 Sample Résumé and Curriculum Vitae	173
Appendix 3 Sample Cover Letter	179
Bibliography	181
Index	189
About the Author	195

List of Figures

Figure 2.1. This is a screenshot of ALA's JobLIST. You can see jobs related to your search and featured jobs that appear regardless of the search criteria entered.   25

Figure 2.2. This is a screenshot of AIM's job board. You can search by category.   27

Figure 2.3. This is a screenshot of LAC Group's job-search page. You can search by category.   27

Figure 2.4. This is a screenshot of Glassdoor's job board. You can click on the entry to see detailed information about the job including reviews of the company.   31

Figure 2.5. This is a screenshot of the LinkedIn groups option. You can click on "DISCOVER MORE" to add additional groups to your LinkedIn profile.   34

Figure 2.6. This is a screenshot of the career-interests section on LinkedIn. Here you can define your career interests and let potential employers know whether you are actively looking.   35

Figure 3.1. This is a sample of how you can organize your files on your computer to make it easier to find application materials later. Within the folder "assistant director," there are two files saved that are related to the application process.   80

List of Tables

Table 1.1.	Types of Positions	2
Table 1.2.	Professional Library Positions	4
Table 1.3.	Some Library Vendors	12
Table 3.1.	Applications Log	82
Table 4.1.	STAR Planning Tool	101
Table 5.1.	Negotiation Criteria	130

Preface

The tremendous growth of information dissemination, collection, and creation, with the explosion of the Internet has created an abundance of library- and information-related jobs in traditional library settings and many other settings you may not expect. *Landing a Library Job* is a guide to help you find and secure one of these jobs.

I have been thinking about writing a book like this since I started developing a course for the undergraduate Information Communication Technology program at the University of Kentucky. No, the class was not about library careers, but it was based on this idea of information work and the transition from an industrial society to an information society. This shift has impacted the types of careers available to library and information science students and workers and how they obtain those jobs.

The shift from an industrial society to an information society has opened a world of new careers that may not have existed even fifteen years ago. This shift has also resulted in a redefining of the purpose and scope of librarians' work and even where they work. Chapter 1 presents jobs suitable for library students and workers, both inside and outside of libraries.

This shift to an information society has also significantly changed how we go about finding and applying for jobs. Chapter 2 starts with a discussion of technologies to aid in your job search. There are sections on using job boards, LISTSERVs, social media, and search engines. The chapter also includes sections on other personal and professional resources for finding jobs and sections on conducting a job search and when to search.

Chapter 3 delves into the application process. This shift to an information-based society has also made its impact on how we apply for jobs and more significantly on the number of people that apply for jobs. The information society has increased the competition level for many jobs. This chapter looks at applying for jobs, focusing on understanding and dissecting the job description and using that information to customize your application materials. A large part of this chapter is dedicated to developing your résumé, curriculum vitae, and a cover letter. And the chapter ends with a section on managing your applications.

Chapter 4 focuses on the interview. The shift to the information society has even impacted how the interview is approached. Employees are expected to know more about the organization, the industry, and so on, even if they have not worked in it. Technology has created new interviewing options. All of this is addressed in this chapter, along with a detailed discussion on preparing for your interview. The chapter includes multiple online resources where you can find library-related interview questions and presents a strategy to help you answer questions under pressure.

While chapter 5 addresses the presence of information societies more subtly (an example would be the thank-you notes section), the information is still crucial for those seeking work in libraries or library-related organizations. This chapter describes important follow-up steps after the interview, including a self-reflection, correspondence, job offers, negotiation, and rejection.

Chapter 6 addresses a key issue for staying relevant in the information society: lifelong learning. This chapter reviews the different types of library degrees, introduces professional certifications, discusses professional-development opportunities (webinars, e-tutorials, etc.), and ends with a section on sharing knowledge.

The end of the book is filled with even more information to assist in your jobs search. Appendix 1 contains a list of almost fifty library or library-related professional associations. The list provides the website and identifies whether the organization has a job board and/or LISTSERVs. The list also identifies whether the organization offers professional certifications. Appendix 2 contains a sample résumé and curriculum vitae used previously by the author. Appendix 3 contains a sample cover letter the author actually used to secure an interview for a library position. You can use both appendixes 2 and 3 as aids when developing your own application materials.

It is my hope that *Landing a Library Job* will give you a renewed excitement for library and library-related jobs across all levels of education and experience and give you the necessary tools and information for finding unique opportunities and distinguishing yourself as a top candidate for those positions.

CHAPTER 1

Identifying Types of Jobs

Working in the library and information science field can be very exciting. Whether you are finishing up a degree in library science, contemplating starting a library or information science program, already working in a library, or some combination of the above, your working future is bright. With experience or education in library and information science you may be able to find employment in a library, a library-related organization, or another emerging information-related profession.

Before setting on your career path or just your next career move (according to the Bureau of Labor Statistics, the average person changes jobs 11.9 times between the ages of eighteen and fifty[1]), you can use the information in this chapter to preview some possible library and library-related jobs that rely and build upon your interest, experience, and knowledge in library and information science. This chapter reviews some traditional library jobs, external library-related employers and positions, and other emerging information-related professions you should consider during your job search. Remember, this is by no means an all-inclusive view of jobs you could land based on your library and information skills and knowledge. The Bureau of Labor Statistics reports that "employment of librarians is projected to grown 9 percent from 2016 to 2026,"[2] and the number of jobs in computer and information technology will grow even more significantly, at 13 percent, from 2016 to 2026,[3] making this field one of the top areas of employment.

LIBRARIES

Traditionally those who studied library and information science worked in libraries, and despite what some predicted at the advent of the Internet there are still plenty of library positions. "According to . . . RSL Research Group, public library staff stood at 139,213 full-time equivalents (FTEs) in 2015, school librarians at 44,623 FTEs in 2015 and academic library staff in 2012 at 85,752 FTEs. In addition, there are thousands of individuals working in medical, law, corporate, government and other types of libraries and archives."[4]

Within these libraries, most employment positions can be grouped according to the expected duties and qualifications of the position. In public, academic, special, and school libraries most positions fall into one of three categories: professional, paraprofessional, and administrative positions (see table 1.1 for examples of each). And while there are

Table 1.1. Types of Positions

Type of Position	Required Education	Sample Duties	Sample Job Titles
Professional	Master of library science degree (preferred) Bachelor's degree (expected)	Oversee library operations Supervise library employees Strategic planning/budgeting Program planning Conduct reference interviews	Library director Assistant director Branch manager Instructional librarian Programming librarian Systems librarian
Paraprofessional	College (preferred) Associate's degree or some college (recommended) Some high school expected and diploma expected in some cases	Reshelve books Check materials out/in Issue library cards Collect fines Data entry Assist with programming	Library assistant Library clerk Library technician Library page
Administrative	Master of library science degree (plus) Bachelor's degree (recommended) Some college (recommended) High school diploma (acceptable and expected in some cases)	Process payroll Maintain employee files Perform general maintenance and cleaning Market programs and services Technology maintenance	Administrative assistant Marketing/social-media coordinator Payroll specialist Human-resources specialist Help desk (IT specialist)

> The Cleveland Clinic libraries nicely exemplify a library (or group of libraries, in this case) that includes multiple examples of each type of library worker: professional, paraprofessional, and administrative. The library has multiple locations and branches serving different Cleveland Clinic locations. The libraries provide services to medical personnel, patients, and other publics and rely on numerous medical librarians, library technicians, a systems librarian, a director, assistant directors, and a department coordinator.[5]

exceptions to these groupings (see later example), understanding these categories can help you during your job search.

Professional library staff refers to positions requiring expert knowledge, formal training, and/or extensive responsibility in a library (e.g., supervision, budgeting, administration, etc.). Various librarians, library managers, library directors, and certified school media specialists are typically considered professional staff. You may be eligible for a professional library position after earning a master's degree in library science and/or significant library experience. *Paraprofessional library staff* refers to positions essential for the daily operations of most libraries, but these positions often require less formalized training and less responsibility, and tend to include more clerical-based tasks. You may be eligible for a paraprofessional position while attending college and/or graduate school. Library technicians and assistants are considered paraprofessional staff. *Administrative-support staff* refers to many other necessary, nonlibrary-related positions in a library. Administrative assistants, security officers, maintenance personnel, employment or marketing specialists, and so on, could all be grouped as administrative-support staff.

Professional Staff

You can find various professional positions in academic, public, and special libraries. Table 1.2 provides a wide-ranging, but not exhaustive, list of some professional library positions with brief descriptions and associated library types (may be more than one).

As you are looking for professional library employment, you will find three predominant functional groups. Administrative professional

Table 1.2. Professional Library Positions

Sample Positions	Brief Description	Library Type	Position Category
School media specialist	Responsible for overall operations of school library	School	Administration, public service, technical service
Library director	Responsible for overall operations of the library	Public, academic, special	Administration
Branch manager	Responsible for overall operations of a specific library branch, and reports to library director	Public, academic, special	Administration
Reference librarian	Assists library users with research and information needs	Public, academic, special	Public service
Children's librarian	Plans and conducts children's programming in the library	Public	Public service
Outreach librarian	Delivers library programming, services, and materials outside the library	Public, academic, special, school	Public service
Instructional librarian	Provides information-literacy instruction	Academic, public	Public service
Cataloging librarian	Responsible for adding and updating catalog records for library resources	Public, academic, special	Technical service
Systems librarian	Responsible for the integrated library system and other digital resources of the library	Public, academic	Technical service

staff are responsible for the overall operations of the library. Library directors, library managers, branch managers, and assistant managers are all considered administrative professional staff. Public-services professional staff are responsible for most of the patron-engaging services. Reference/information, outreach, programming, and instruction are some types of public services that may be found in different types of libraries. Technical-services professional staff work behind the scenes to make sure the library can provide adequate services to patrons.

> A school media specialist is an example of a professional library position that combines multiple positions. The school media specialist can be found in school libraries and typically serves as the head librarian and technical and public-services librarian. As a school media specialist you would likely be responsible for collection development, circulation, book fairs, volunteers, etc., and report to the school's principal and possibly someone at the district level. Some school media specialists may also serve as the technology expert in their school. In most states you would need specialized training in education, library resources, and programming to work as a school media specialist (see chapter 6 for more details).

Technical-services professional areas include acquisitions, cataloging, systems administration, and so on.

These positions are not always independent of each other. In some libraries multiple professional library positions may be combined based on librarian interests/skills or the library size or structure. In other libraries, librarian positions may be outsourced or coordinated by a state association or consortium.

Administration

You will likely need to have extensive library experience and at least a master's degree in library science to work in library administration. Occasionally exceptions are made, but more often than not you would need both to qualify for these types of positions. Some of the most common library-administration positions include library directors, library managers, branch managers, and assistant directors. Below is a brief description of each.

- *Library directors* are responsible for all library operations. Library directors can be found in academic, public, and special libraries—although special libraries may use the terms "library director" and "library manager" interchangeably. As a library director you would need a general understanding of all aspects of the library. In addition to library coursework or experience on collection management, reference, technology resources, etc., you would need to have coursework and/or experience in personnel management, financial planning/budgeting, customer/employee relations, public affairs/relations, and even building management. You would manage a team of professional, paraprofessional, and administrative staff who assist in carrying out the day-to-day operations.

- *Library managers* are often librarians with additional supervisory and/or oversight responsibilities. Library managers are less common than librarians and are seldom found in small libraries but may be quite common in larger libraries, especially academic and public libraries. As a library manager you may directly supervise employees and daily operations for a particular department (e.g., circulation, reference, acquisitions, etc.), oversee programming and special projects, and serve on the library's management team.
- *Branch managers* are similar to both library managers and library directors in that they take on the management/administrative responsibilities for their particular location. As a branch manager you would directly supervise library employees and the daily operations for a designated branch and typically serve on the overall library's management team. As a branch manager you may also be responsible for managing the branch's budget and overseeing its maintenance. Branch managers are different from library managers in that they may need to be familiar with many aspects/functions of the library instead of being an expert in one particular area of the library. They are different from library directors in that they do not represent or make decisions for the entire library organization.
- One or more *assistant directors* can be found in some libraries. As an assistant director you may serve as a library manager for a particular aspect of the library, or you may need a general understanding of all aspects of the library. You would work closely with the director and be prepared to step in should the director step down for any reason. You would likely need education and experience in library management in addition to knowledge specific to library services and processes.

Public Services

Public services encompasses many of the patron-focused services in the library. These include providing reference, outreach, programming, and instruction services, just to name a few. If you have taken classes or have experience in reference and information services, information literacy, information searching, children's and young-adult literature and programming, or outreach services, then you may be a good fit for a public-service library position. Below are some examples of public-service positions in libraries.

- *Reference and information librarians* may be found in academic, public, and special libraries. School media specialists may perform the duties of a reference librarian as needed. Reference and information librarians are responsible for helping library users find essential information and resources (both through the library and externally) to fulfill their information need. If you have a desire to help people solve problems and enjoy looking for information, then you may be a good fit for a reference and information librarian.
- *Outreach services* are traditionally found in public libraries but can also be found in academic, special, and school libraries. Outreach services include bookmobile services, daycare programs, and other offsite and engagement library services in libraries. If you have a desire to go out in the community and engage patrons in their space or if you have a particular interest in working with children, older adults, or underrepresented populations, then you may thrive in an outreach program at a library.
- *Programming* is a broad category for the planning and execution of activities and events in a library. Programming staff may focus on a particular population as their primary focus, or they may provide general programming for the entire library. If you have an interest and/or experience in event planning, working with a designated population (e.g., children, adults, teenagers, etc.), and coordinating staff-wide events, then you may thrive as a programming librarian. Programming librarians must have good

organizational, time-management, delegation, and communication (specifically presentation) skills.
- Similar to, and in some libraries even grouped with, programming services is the *instructional-/information-literacy librarian*. Instructional-/information-literacy services are typically found in all four types of libraries. Services that fall into this realm include one-on-one instruction, reference interviews, and technology and information workshops/tutorials, among others. If you have an interest or education in information literacy, emerging technologies and information resources, and teaching, then you may thrive as an instructional librarian.

Technical Services

Technical services are significant in all types of libraries, often occur out of the public eye, and require minimal interaction with patrons. If you took classes related to automated library systems, Web technologies, cataloging and classification, or collection development, technical services might be of interest to you. Below are some examples of technical-services positions in libraries.

- *Cataloging* is essential for the organization of library resources and providing better service to patrons. The level of cataloging activities may vary depending on the type and size of the library. Some large libraries may have staff dedicated to different materials. For example, they may have someone or a department dedicated to processing periodicals and one for nonfiction, reference, and fiction books. Other large libraries organize cataloging departments based on tasks. Updating/entering cataloging records and preparing books for shelving may be examples of some of the cataloging duties. If you are detail-oriented, have a passion for organization, and have training in cataloging and/or classification systems then you may thrive as a cataloging librarian.
- *Acquisitions* is the procurement of digital and physical inventory for the library. No matter how large or small the library, acquisitions is an important part for all libraries. Larger libraries may have a whole department devoted to acquisitions with

collection-development librarians, electronic-resources librarians, and other library staff. Some libraries may have one librarian as its acquisitions department. And still other libraries may not have a dedicated acquisitions librarian or department but rather divide the acquisition duties among multiple library staff in other departments. If you have an interest and/or education in collection development, databases, or even cataloging then you may thrive as an acquisitions librarian.

- *Systems administration* is crucial to the operation of almost any library. Without an integrated library system (ILS) or some technological components, libraries may struggle to provide adequate services for their populations. Most medium to large libraries have at least one librarian or staff member who spends at least part of their time managing the ILS. Many small to medium libraries may rely on outsourcing or parent or affiliated organizations to assist in systems administration, or they may not even use an ILS. If you have a background in ILS or other library technologies then you may thrive as a systems librarian.

Paraprofessional Staff

Paraprofessional staff are essential to running most libraries. These support positions are typically held by individuals with various levels of education but who do not hold a professional library degree. Common paraprofessional positions may include library technicians or assistants and other administrative support staff. You may be eligible to work in some of these roles with a high school diploma, bachelor's degree, associate's degree, or specific certification. Some school and special libraries may even utilize volunteer paraprofessional staff and so may be more flexible on the requirements. Paraprofessional staff are typically grouped based on education/training requirements and/or function.

Education/Training Requirements

Most library-technician positions require a minimum of a high school diploma or GED, while many require a postsecondary certificate or degree (see chapter 6 for more information about certificates and degrees) with coursework in library processes such as "acquisitions, cataloging, circulation, reference, and automated library systems." Library assistants are typically required to have a minimum of a high school diploma or GED and receive short-term on-the-job training to familiarize them with library-specific tasks and terminology.[6]

Function

Both library technicians and assistants perform a variety of clerical, customer-service, and support tasks. Library size and workforce qualifications and experience may impact how technicians and assistants are assigned work. For example, in a small library a technician and assistant may share many of the same duties. In a larger library support staff may be divided based on education or experience. For example, technicians may be the preferred hire for a cataloging department since they may have education related to formatting and updating electronic library records. The same library may rely on a library assistant to help patrons at the circulation or information desk. Regardless, whether a library technician or assistant is working in a public area, a technical area, or both, they are expected to have good interpersonal-communication skills, be detail-oriented, and understand basic technologies.

Administrative-Support Staff

An administrative assistant, security officer, maintenance technician, employment specialist, or marketing specialist could be classified as administrative support staff because their work is essential to the library but does not require education/experience specific to libraries. Due to the variety of tasks administrative-support staff perform, their educational requirements may vary greatly. For example, a maintenance technician may not be required to hold a high school diploma but may be expected to have experience in maintenance processes. An administrative assistant may be required to have a high school diploma or some college, depending on the specific library's expectations. Often an employment or marketing specialist might be required to have college work (or degree) or experience in their respective field. If your undergraduate education or work experience falls into one of the administrative-support areas you may consider applying for these types of positions while pursuing library science coursework or starting your professional journey in librarianship.

EXTERNAL LIBRARY-RELATED POSITIONS

As you are seeking employment, don't forget about organizations that serve libraries. Library vendors and parent or other partner organizations of libraries are both viable employment options for you. Since these organizations work closely with libraries you can use your knowledge and/or experience in libraries as a selling feature in your application.

Library Vendors

If you are a library worker or a library student willing and even eager to explore library-related opportunities outside of libraries, working for a library vendor may be an excellent career path for you. Libraries depend on various vendors to provide services and operate the library effectively. Many of these vendors provide goods or services to multiple libraries across the country (and globe) and can benefit from employees who understand how libraries operate. Table 1.3 lists common products and services that libraries may outsource and some providers of those services. This list can be a good place to start your extended job search. You may also be able to find additional vendors by inquiring with individual libraries about their vendors or by searching the different product and service categories listed in table 1.3.

Publishers

The publishing industry employed over 420,000 people in 2017 as sales agents, editors, graphic designers, reporters, and correspondents.[7] As a library science student or library employee your skills and knowledge can be applied to a number of positions found with publishers or distributors of books. Sales representatives or account managers are two common publishing-industry positions that could utilize some of

Table 1.3. Some Library Vendors

Traditional publishers and book suppliers	Baker & Taylor
	Ingram Content Group
	Pearson
	Cengage
	HarperCollins
	Scholastic Corporation
Electronic resources (e.g., e-books, databases, etc.)	ProQuest
	Cengage
	Recorded Books
	EBSCO Information Services
Integrated library systems	Ex Libris Group
	The Library Corporation (TLC)
	OCLC
	SirsiDynix
Security systems	3M
	Schlage
	Honeywell
Library supplies	Demco, Inc.
	3M
	Gaylord
	Kingsley
	Brodart
Other	LibSynergy LLC
	TechSoup

your knowledge and skills in librarianship. The "library market now represents just over 1.3 percent of publisher's trade sales."[8] While this does not seem like much, it is still significant enough to need sales representatives and account managers that are familiar with libraries.

If sales and account management do not appeal to you but you have an interest in the publishing industry, there are many other positions in the publishing industry that can benefit from your library training and experience. Beyond sales, Bookjobs.com has identified eighteen additional employment areas in the publishing industry: administrative, advertising, audio, art and design, editorial, finance, human resources, information technology, Internet development, legal contracts, managing editorial, marketing, production, promotion, publicity, publisher's office, purchasing, and subsidiary rights and permissions.[9]

Technology

Libraries rely on a number of technology products/services to manage the library and serve patrons. One of the primary products many libraries depend on is an integrated library management system. ILS systems, as they are known, are used in circulation, inventory management, processing patron records, and reporting, among many other functions. Companies that specialize in these types of systems (e.g., The Library Corporation, Innovative Interfaces, Ex Libris Group) deal with many libraries and can often benefit from hiring library workers or library science graduates who are familiar with the unique industry and its needs. If you have a technical understanding of and experience or education in library systems you may be able to work in technical services or support. If you are less technical but know the valuable role these systems play in libraries, you could be a sales consultant or customer-relations associate.

Libraries provide a lot of access to information online for their patrons. Many libraries subscribe to electronic databases usually of interest to their patrons. For example, some public libraries subscribe to ChiltonDIY, a database of auto-repair information currently owned by Cengage.[10] School or academic libraries may subscribe to ProQuest, a general database that provides access to scholarly journals, newspapers, reports, working papers, data sets, digitized historical primary sources, and more than 450,000 e-books.[11] Legal libraries or law firms may subscribe to LexisNexis, a database of full-text documents from legal resources (e.g., newspapers, journals, court decisions, etc.). All of these database companies could be potential employers. You could look for positions in sales, customer service, or technical support depending on your background.

Parent and Other Affiliated Organizations

Most libraries are not stand-alone entities. More often than not a library is connected to at least one other organization. Those organizations might be a parent organization—such as a government agency, corporation, university, or school system—or those organizations might be affiliated organizations—such as cooperatives, consortiums, professional associations, government agencies, or other nonprofit organizations. Many of these organizations may offer library- and information-related employment opportunities. This next section will review some of the different types of organizations and potential positions within those organizations.

Parent Organizations

The level of involvement or authority of a parent organization over a library may vary depending on the type of library. Some common parent organizations include government, corporations, universities/colleges, and school systems.

Many public libraries receive funding from taxpayer dollars. As such those same libraries are governed by a board appointed by the local government. The board serves as an oversight committee for the public library's expenditures, hiring practices, etc.

If you are interested in public service, government departments or agencies (local, state, federal) may be a good addition to your job search. Many government departments or agencies are responsible for maintaining, updating, or disposing of records or developing/maintaining online information portals. These are all responsibilities where your library science background could make you excel.

Many special libraries are a part of larger corporations or entities. You know that many hospitals and law firms house libraries, but did you know television stations, factories, and a host of other corporations maintain collections as well? And not only are those libraries potential places for employment, but there are also other departments within those corporations. For example the sales department may have a customer-relationship management system that needs to be updated, maintained, and supported. Or the human-resources department may have an employee database or personnel records to maintain. These departments and many others can benefit from your library and information science skills and knowledge.

Many colleges and universities have at least one library, and some have multiple libraries. Each of the libraries must adhere to the college's or university's policies and procedures related to student records, faculty services, circulation policies, etc.

In addition to libraries, colleges and universities provide a wealth of additional employment opportunities suitable for library science students and library workers. You could work in enterprise management, student-records management, student affairs, and educational technology, among other areas. Many positions in higher education require at least a master's degree, and a master's degree in library science can prove to be incredibly beneficial.

> Academic advisors and student-affairs personnel in many colleges and universities are required to have at least a master's degree. A master's in library science is a good match for many of these positions. Academic advisors and student-affairs personnel must display exceptional customer-service skills, value privacy, update and maintain student and departmental records, and guide students to campus resources.

School libraries or media centers must adhere to both school regulations and district regulations. Schools and districts often manage expenditures, student records, selection of materials, etc. These are all areas where library science skills and training could benefit.

If you have an interest in K–12 education but don't want to be in the classroom or lack the appropriate credentials to teach or serve as librarian, there are still a number of other positions in the school district and/or the schools you could pursue. You could search for positions in data and evaluation, records management, and technology, among other areas.

Affiliated Organizations

Affiliated organizations could be cooperatives or consortiums, professional associations, or governing bodies that regulate or represent libraries. Below are some examples of the different types of affiliated organizations. This is not an exhaustive list. You should check with libraries in your area to learn about some additional affiliated organizations.

- *Cooperatives and consortiums* are popular among libraries because they allow libraries to share resources and costs while providing improved services to patrons. Many of these organizations are managed independently of participating libraries and employ their own staff. The positions may range from administrative positions (e.g., human resources, finance, public relations, etc.) to library consultants to librarians.
- *Library and library-related professional associations* may exist at the international, national, state, and regional levels. Many national and international library associations are named in ap-

> Kentucky Virtual Library (KYVL) is a consortium providing database access, courier service, and the Kentucky Digital Library platform to almost three hundred member libraries and institutions. This particular consortium employs three support staff as director, senior fellow, and business specialist.[12] OCLC, on the other hand, is an example of a large library-related cooperative; they have nineteen offices across eleven countries[13] providing technology services to thousands of libraries.[14]

pendix 1. As the label implies, professional associations exist to provide professional development, lobbying, guidance, and other services for its members (individual and/or institutional). Many professional organizations operate with minimal staff in administrative and operational (marketing, human resources, etc.) types of positions.

- Some *libraries and library-related organizations* may be required to abide by certain financial, records-management, and employee-relations regulations. Many states have state libraries that enforce and mandate these regulations for public libraries. Additionally, these state libraries may also provide financial, professional-development, and other types of support. The Kentucky Department for Libraries and Archives, Tennessee State Library and Archives, and the Texas State Library and Archives Commission, along with agencies for other states, operate the division of library services and archives and records management for their respective states.

OTHER POTENTIAL LIBRARY AND INFORMATION SCIENCE OCCUPATIONS

While libraries, library vendors, and other library-related organizations offer exciting employment opportunities for you, the growth of computer technology and information sharing has led to even more career options for library and information science students and professionals. The Association of Information Science and Technology (ASIS&T) has identified seven other "occupational groups within the information professions" beyond libraries.[15] Depending on your interests, educational program, and experience you may want to incorporate the ASIS&T–identified occupational paths as part of your job search.

Archives and Records Management

Regardless of whether a business or organization uses the terms archives and records management, it likely still must address the maintenance of customer and employee records. Many industries have policies about how long to keep records and privacy concerns associated with those records. If you have taken library and information science coursework related to archives- and records-management experience or have experience in maintaining records this occupational path may be a good fit for you.

Computer Engineering

Library science students and professionals have not traditionally been top candidates in the computer-engineering field, but changes in library and information science curriculum and practices have made many library science students and professionals better prepared to take on certain roles in the computer-engineering occupation. If you have taken library and information science coursework in technology services, computer programming, or other computer engineering–related topics, or if you have experience with makerspaces such as digital studios or 3-D printers, then this occupational path may be a good fit for you.

Data Analysis and Research

Due to the tremendous amount of data generated and collected through online interactions (e.g., online shopping, online dating, online banking, social-media sharing, etc.), there is a growing need for people trained in and familiar with analyzing data. If you completed coursework in databases (e.g., Microsoft Access, SQL), database visualization (e.g., Tableau) or data mining as part of your library and information science curriculum, have an understanding of relational databases and statistical analysis, or experience in compiling and analyzing usage data then this occupational path may be a good fit for you.

Informatics and Information Science

The study of the use and application of information and technology is increasingly important as our world continues to become more digital. Many businesses, organizations, and even governments are involved in the integration of new technologies. This includes everything from designing and deploying the technology to implementing policies and laws related to the technology to studying the effects of the technology. If you have an interest in ethical or legal uses of technology, have training in assessing technologies, or have education in informatics then this occupational path may be a good fit for you.

Metadata/Indexing/Taxonomy

While metadata, indexing, and taxonomy have all traditionally been part of library and information science education, the explosion of the Internet and technologies like social tagging and search-engine optimization have created a new need for those trained in these areas. If you have an interest in or understanding of describing and classifying data and information then this occupational path may be a good fit for you.

Information Architecture, User Experience, and Web Design

The need for customers, employees, government agencies, and other bodies to access and share electronic information has led to the development and growth of information-architecture, user-experience, and Web-design jobs. If you have education in information organization and design principles and/or experience in Web design or content-management systems then this occupational path may be a good fit for you.

Information Management

Technology has created many challenges and opportunities related to the capture, storage, sharing, preservation, and delivery of institutional information. If you have experience, education, or interest in designing applications and solutions to manage the information flow in an organization then this occupational path may be a good fit for you.

NOTES

1. Bureau of Labor Statistics, "Number of Jobs Held, Labor Market Activity, and Earnings Growth among the Youngest Baby Boomers: Results from a Longitudinal Survey Summary," Economic News Release, United States Department of Labor, August 24, 2017, https://www.bls.gov/news.release/nlsoy.nr0.htm.

2. Bureau of Labor Statistics, "Librarians," *Occupational Outlook Handbook*, US Department of Labor, last modified July 2, 2018, https://www.bls.gov/ooh/education-training-and-library/librarians.htm.

3. Bureau of Labor Statistics, "Computer and Information Technology Occupations," *Occupational Outlook Handbook*, United States Department of Labor, last modified April 13, 2018, https://www.bls.gov/ooh/computer-and-information-technology/home.htm.

4. James Neal (@jamesneal), Twitter post, December 29, 2017, 1:25 PM, https://twitter.com/jamesneal/status/946854738435411968.

5. Cleveland Clinic, "Library Staff and Mission," accessed December 7, 2018, https://portals.clevelandclinic.org/library/About-the-Library/Library-Staff-Mission.

6. Bureau of Labor Statistics, "Library Technicians and Assistants," *Occupational Outlook Handbook*, United States Department of Labor, last modified April 13, 2018, https://www.bls.gov/ooh/education-training-and-library/mobile/library-technicians-and-assistants.htm.

7. Bureau of Labor Statistics, "Publishing Industries (Except Internet): NAICS 511," Industries at a Glance, United States Department of Labor, accessed October 30, 2018, https://www.bls.gov/iag/tgs/iag511.htm.

8. David Vinjamuri, "The Case for Libraries," *Publishers Weekly*, April 3, 2015, https://www.publishersweekly.com/pw/by-topic/industry-news/libraries/article/66106-the-case-for-libraries.html.

9. Bookjobs.com, "Major/Department Guide," Association of American Publishers, Inc., accessed September 20, 2018, http://www.bookjobs.com/major-to-department-guide.

10. Chilton, "About Us," accessed September 7, 2018, http://www.chilton.cengage.com/home/about.

11. ProQuest, "Databases," accessed September 7, 2018, https://www.proquest.com/products-services/databases/.

12. Kentucky Virtual Library, "About KYVL," last updated November 6, 2018, https://www.kyvl.org/about.

13. OCLC, "Discover. Innovate. Collaborate. Inform. Make a Meaningful Difference at OCLC: Who We Are," Careers, accessed September 26, 2018, https://www.oclc.org/en/careers.html.

14. OCLC, "Together We Make Breakthroughs Possible," About, accessed September 26, 2018, https://www.oclc.org/en/about.html.

15. Association for Information Science and Technology, "Occupational Paths," accessed July 7, 2018, https://www.asist.org/careers/occupational-paths/.

BIBLIOGRAPHY

Association for Information Science and Technology. "Occupational Paths." Accessed July 7, 2018. https://www.asist.org/careers/occupational-paths/.

Bookjobs.com. "Major/Department Guide." Association of American Publishers, Inc. Accessed September 20, 2018. http://www.bookjobs.com/major-to-department-guide.

Bureau of Labor Statistics. "Computer and Information Technology Occupations." *Occupational Outlook Handbook*. United States Department of Labor. Last modified April 13, 2018. https://www.bls.gov/ooh/computer-and-information-technology/home.htm.

———. "Librarians." *Occupational Outlook Handbook*. United States Department of Labor. Last modified July 2, 2018. https://www.bls.gov/ooh/education-training-and-library/librarians.htm.

———. "Library Technicians and Assistants." *Occupational Outlook Handbook*. United States Department of Labor. Last modified April 13, 2018. https://www.bls.gov/ooh/education-training-and-library/mobile/library-technicians-and-assistants.htm.

———. "Number of Jobs Held, Labor Market Activity, and Earnings Growth among the Youngest Baby Boomers: Results from a Longitudinal Survey Summary." Economic News Release. United States Department of Labor. August 24, 2017. https://www.bls.gov/news.release/nlsoy.nr0.htm.

———. "Publishing Industries (Except Internet): NAICS 511." Industries at a Glance. United States Department of Labor. Accessed October 30, 2018. https://www.bls.gov/iag/tgs/iag511.htm.

Chilton. "About Us." Accessed September 7, 2018. http://www.chilton.cengage.com/home/about.

Cleveland Clinic. "Library Staff and Mission." Accessed December 7, 2018. https://portals.clevelandclinic.org/library/About-the-Library/Library-Staff-Mission.

Kentucky Virtual Library. "About KYVL." Last updated November 6, 2018. https://www.kyvl.org/about.

Neal, James (@jamesneal). Twitter Post. December 29, 2017, 1:25 PM. https://twitter.com/jamesneal/status/946854738435411968.

OCLC. "Discover. Innovate. Collaborate. Inform. Make a Meaningful Difference at OCLC: Who We Are." Careers. Accessed September 26, 2018. https://www.oclc.org/en/careers.html.

———. "Together We Make Breakthroughs Possible." About. Accessed September 26, 2018. https://www.oclc.org/en/about.html.

ProQuest. "Databases." Accessed September 7, 2018. https://www.proquest.com/products-services/databases/.

Vinjamuri, David. "The Case for Libraries." *Publishers Weekly*. April 3, 2015. https://www.publishersweekly.com/pw/by-topic/industry-news/libraries/article/66106-the-case-for-libraries.html.

CHAPTER 2

Finding Jobs

Are you getting ready to graduate with a degree in library and information science? Are you considering a career change in library and information science? You can use the information in this chapter to help you on your job search. This chapter will introduce some tools and techniques for finding work both inside and outside of libraries, discuss terminology and parameters to use in your job search, and address when you should apply.

WHERE TO LOOK

The US Department of Labor reported 6.3 million jobs were open in January 2018,[1] and the number of library jobs is projected to increase 9 percent between 2016 and 2026.[2] This section will identify some of the online tools and techniques to help you find and apply for library and library-related jobs.

ONLINE TOOLS

The Bureau of Labor Statistics claims "the online job search (OJS)... is now the most popular method of jobhunting,"[3] and library and information science work is no exception. This section will discuss online job boards, LISTSERVs, social media, and job search engines that can be used during the job search for both library and library-related jobs.

Job Boards

All job boards serve job seekers by displaying select job announcements. Some job boards allow applicants to apply directly from the job board and manage the application process as additional services. Job boards may be managed by professional associations, placement agencies (library-specific or other industries), the employing library or library-related organization, or general job boards. You should plan to visit and use a variety of job boards to increase your employment opportunities.

There are a number of professional associations important for those interested in library or library-related work. During your job search you should identify those professional associations most closely aligned with your career goals.

There are benefits to identifying and using professional-association job boards during your search.

1. Using professional-association job boards reduces your need to search the vast Internet. Professional associations list library or library-related jobs in one central location.
2. Using professional-association job boards reduces your worry about the legitimacy of a job announcement or potential employer. Many professional-association job boards require libraries or library-related organizations to pay or be a member to post job announcements. Others may have an approval process, meaning the job board verifies the employer before posting the job. However, this does not mean that all professional job boards approve job postings. You should see the specific job board's policies regarding job postings to confirm their policy.
3. Indicating you learned of a job opening through a respected professional-association job board conveys to the hiring official you are knowledgeable about the library and information science field.

Placement agencies devoted to library and library-related job searches may be few in number but are large in impact. AIM and Lib-Gig are two popular library and information placement agencies with

One popular professional association with a large library-related job board is the American Library Association. ALA's job board is open and free to use by anyone looking for library or select library–related jobs. You can access the ALA's job board by visiting http://www.ala.org and clicking on "More Jobs" under the header "Featured Jobs | ALA JobLIST" at the bottom of the web page. Once on the job board, you can search by keyword, job title, and/or location. After conducting the initial search you can further limit your search by sorting by position, company, location, or posted date. You can also elect to filter based on organization type, primary job function, job type, or state. Upon finding a position you are interested in, you can save the position to apply later. You can also set up alerts by clicking on the "E-mail Me Jobs like This" button.

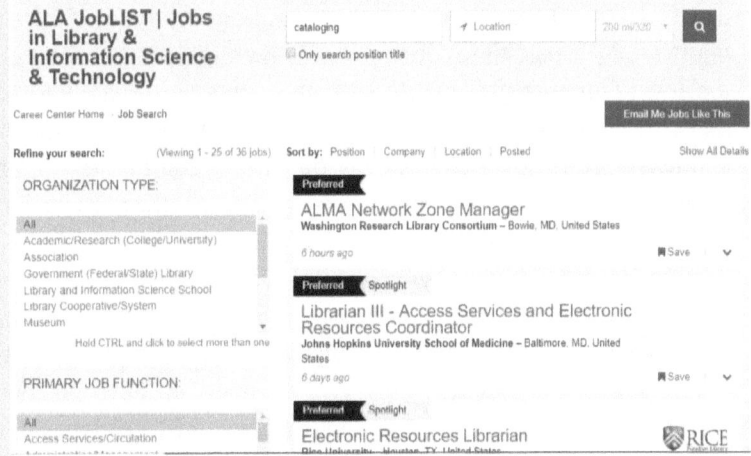

Fig. 2.1.   You can see jobs related to your search and featured jobs that appear regardless of the search criteria entered.
ALA, screenshot

The Association of Information Science and Technology (ASIS&T) is another professional association website you can use to search for library jobs or positions in the other seven occupational paths identified by ASIS&T (presented in chapter 1). You can search by keyword, job title, and/or location. You can further sort by position, company, or location, and you can filter by job function, industry, and state. You can also sign up to receive e-mails when similar jobs are posted. This job site, like ALA, is powered by YM Careers, so they are set up identically.

These are just some examples of library and library-related professional associations. See appendix 1 for a more extensive list of library and library-related professional associations that have job boards. Keep in mind that many of the professional associations charge a fee to join but may offer freely accessible job-board access for job seekers. The level of access may be restricted or limited to only viewing (instead of applying) positions on the free job board.

job boards. You should plan to include both of these job boards as part of your job search.

- AIM Library & Information Staffing places librarians and support staff specifically in jobs in "special, public, academic, school, government libraries and information centers."[4] You can visit https://www.aimusa.com and click on "JOB SEEKERS/EMPLOYEES" or "HOT JOBS" to see a list of current job announcements. The announcements are listed in chronological order by posting date but can be sorted alphabetically by job title, organization, city, or state. Or you can elect to group positions by type of library, hours (full- or part-time), hire status (direct hire or temporary), or job level (support staff or MLS/MLIS degree required). You can apply directly from the AIM Library & Information Staffing site, and by registering you get priority on current and future jobs and consideration for all applicable jobs posted on the website (see figure 2.2).[5]
- LibGig is a LAC Group company and tool for librarians and others interested in library, information, and knowledge professions. You can visit https://www.libgig.com to search and apply for library and library-related jobs. You can view all open positions or search by job function, location, or keyword (see figure 2.3). Then you can read descriptions and apply for positions direct from the LibGig website. A recruiter will follow up with you when they believe your credentials are a good match for the job opening.

Using a placement agency affords many of the same benefits of professional-association job boards and some additional benefits. One of the most significant is the direct recommendation to the employer. Many placement agencies—AIM and LibGig not excluded—initially screen the applicants before releasing them to the employer. If you are referred by a placement agency then you know you are likely among the top candidates for the position. San José State University's School of Information identifies multiple other benefits of using a placement agency. Gaining experience, increasing your network, boosting your confidence, developing professional references familiar with your work abilities, and possible future permanent em-

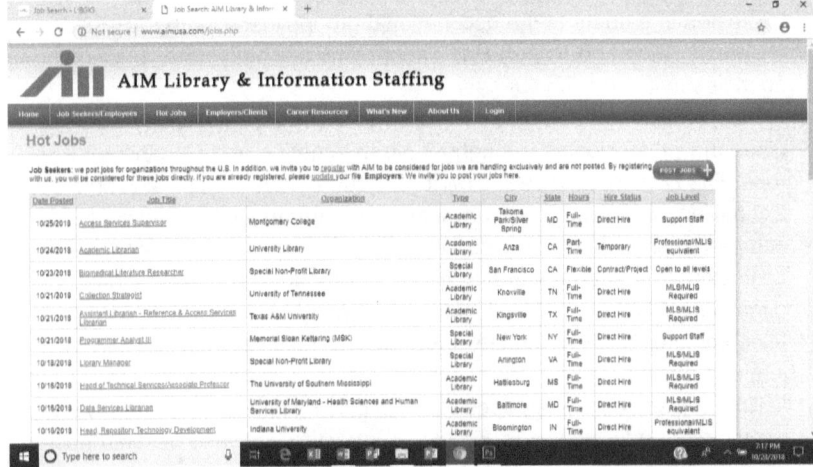

Fig. 2.2. You can search by category.
AIMUSA, screenshot

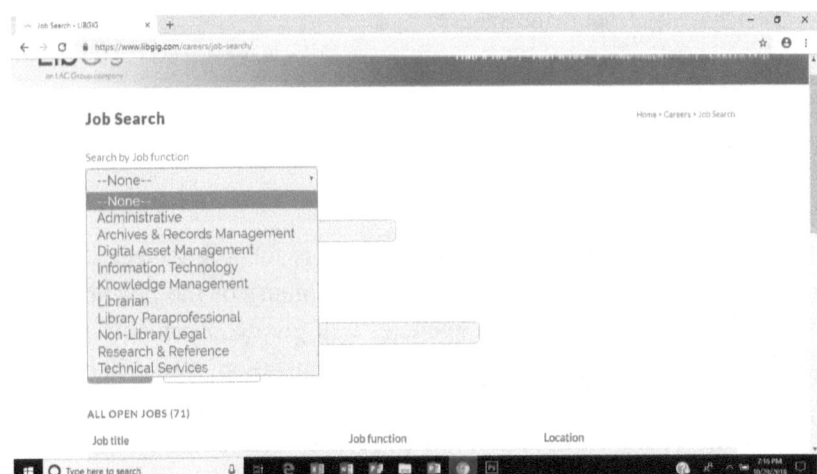

Fig. 2.3. You can search by category.
LAC Group, screenshot

> AIM and LibGig are not the only placement agencies that may be of interest to you as a library and information science professional. If you are interested in careers in the occupational groups identified by ASIS&T in chapter 1, Dice and Robert Half Technology are both viable placement agencies to include in your search.
>
> Dice provides specialized recruiting services for technology and engineering professionals throughout North America and Continental Europe. The Dice website sees 2 million unique visitors monthly and houses 2.2 million websites.[6] You can search by job title, skills, keywords, or company name. You can also search by zip code, city, or state. After conducting the search you can filter by company segment (recruiter or direct hire), distance, title, location, company, employment type, and telecommute. You can create a job alert to receive e-mails when new jobs are posted.
>
> Robert Half Technology specializes in placing information-science and technology professionals in "project, contract-to-hire, and full-time positions."[7] You can search for open positions by keyword and/or location. Then you can filter by staffing area, location (city and miles), employment types, and posting date or sort by relevance. After conducting a search you can subscribe to job alerts to receive e-mails when a new position is posted that matches your search. You can also elect to "simply upload your résumé or LinkedIn profile," and Robert Half will work to find positions that match your credentials.[8]

ployment are among the most significant benefits as you are starting your job search.[9]

1. *Gaining experience.* Whether the job is for a few weeks, a few months, a few years, or permanently, many of the positions offered through placement agencies will give you valuable experience in a library or library-related organization. You will be able to add this experience to your résumé. You can even highlight some of the skills and knowledge you were able to further develop through this experience.
2. *Increasing your network.* You will make new connections in the library or library-related organization and its partner organizations (e.g., nearby libraries, state associations, vendors, etc.) you engage during your placement. Be sure to keep a list of those

connections and reach out to them when applicable to your job or to seek guidance about applying for positions similar to their positions or in the same organization.
3. *Boosting your confidence.* The more practice you get in your field, the more confident you will become, and the more it will show in your interviews. You will be able to share current and relevant examples of your experience when asked behavioral interview questions (see chapter 4 for more on this topic).
4. *Developing professional references familiar with your work abilities.* While on assignment (temporary or permanent) you will report to and interact with professionals in the library or library-related organization as coworkers, supervisors, supervisees, etc. Be sure to ask those you work closely with about serving as references and get their current contact information (regardless of their level in the organization). Those you do not work closely with may still be significant. Be sure to record at least their names and titles because you may still be able to connect with them through tools like LinkedIn or professional associations.
5. *Potential future employment.* Accepting a position through a placement agency may likely lead to future employment in a couple of different ways. First, many libraries or library-related organizations use temporary employment to try out an employee before offering full-time employment. If the position is permanent you may be offered full-time employment if the library or library-related organization finds your work suitable. Second, if you perform satisfactorily on a temporary assignment the placement agency may continue to recommend you for positions with its other clients.

Many individual libraries and library-related employers house job boards on their own websites. These boards may be open to the general public or restricted to current employees. The most basic of these boards may include a simple list of open positions with application information. Others may provide much more automated services by providing searching or filtering services based on location, department, or other criteria and an online application process. Either way, this may be your most successful way to find and apply for positions at many small libraries that may not have funding to post job announcements on pay sites.

> Many libraries have their own websites, but since some libraries are part of larger organizations (e.g., universities, school districts, hospitals, etc.), open library positions are posted on the employer's website, not directly on the library's website. This is very common for school libraries or school-media centers, who are governed by a school district. For example, on September 6, 2018, Hite Elementary School in Louisville, Kentucky, posted a library media-specialist position in the Jefferson County Public Schools employment system.[10] Even though the school has its own library website, the school is part of a larger school district that oversees all hiring.

General job boards cater to job seekers in both the public and private sectors in a variety of industries. However vast, these tools should not be overlooked. General job boards can highlight some unique opportunities for those with library and information science degrees or experience, especially if you are looking for some of the jobs outside libraries. CareerBuilder, ZipRecruiter, and Glassdoor are among the most popular general job boards and offer additional benefits you may not find on other job boards.

- CareerBuilder is a global job and talent finder that serves about three thousand employers worldwide and partners with three hundred companies to post three million monthly jobs.[11] You can search the massive job bank, save your résumé, and access a beta tool called My Career Path. When you conduct a job search you can search by location (city, state, or zip-code), job title, skills, or company. You can also browse postings from the home screen. The top browsing criteria are by category, city, and company. Once you conduct a search you can sort by relevance, date, or company. You can also filter by posting date, type of employment, salary, company, job category, and/or whether or not you can apply through CareerBuilder. Once you conduct a job search you can sign up for job alerts on the search you conduct. By signing up for the job search you can get weekly or daily updates on new positions that meet your search. The job alerts sync with any filters you set up.

- ZipRecruiter was started as a recruiting tool for small businesses, and by 2010 it evolved into an organization serving over 1 million employers and 120 million job seekers.[12] You can search by job title or keyword and by city, state, or zip-code. Then you can filter based on distance, salary, employment type, job title, and company. When you apply directly on ZipRecruiter's website the system will keep you posted as you go through the hiring process.
- Glassdoor is a job board that has unique extras for you as a job seeker. You can search for jobs, read company reviews posted by employees, and "see CEO approval ratings, salary reports, interview review and questions, benefits reviews, office photos, and more."[13] You can search by job title, keywords, or company. If you are not certain what to search for, you can browse popular searches, jobs (by category or field), city, and salaries. After searching you can further filter your search by type of job, time, salary range, distance, city, industry, company, size, and company rating. Company rating is significantly unique to Glassdoor, as employees can create Glassdoor accounts and share reviews and other information about employers. You can read this information before you apply for a position (see figure 2.4).

Fig. 2.4. *You can click on the entry to see detailed information about the job including reviews of the company.*
Glassdoor, screenshot

LISTSERVs

As you are looking for employment you should consider subscribing to multiple LISTSERVs related to your area of interest. Many professional associations, library schools, and other organizations have LISTSERVs you can join. For many professional associations there may be a fee to join the association, but sometimes you can join the LISTSERV for free.

There are also some LISTSERVs dedicated specifically to those looking for employment in the library and information field. This section includes two LISTSERVs and how to subscribe to those lists. You can find information about other LISTSERVs in appendix 1.

The International Federation of Library Associations and Institutions (IFLA) offers over ninety mailing lists. Since 1995 IFLA has offered a library and information science jobs mailing list. It is called libjobs@infoserv.inist.fr. To subscribe to this list, visit http://www.ifla.org/mailing-lists and scroll down until you see "LIBJOBS" in the list. Click on "SUBSCRIBE." Then enter your e-mail address, and click "SUBMIT." You will then receive an e-mail with a password you should enter on the confirmation page. Should you decide to unsubscribe from this list, revisit http://www.ifla.org/mailing-lists, find "LIBJOBS," click on "UNSUBSCRIBE," and follow the on-screen instructions. If you are not logged in you will be prompted to enter your password.

The American Library Association (ALA) has a number of electronic mailing lists. Some are open to members only, and some are open to everyone. Their LISTSERV rssjcr-l@lists.ala.org includes job announcements and workshop offerings, among other things. To subscribe, visit http://lists.ala.org, and click on the list options menu. Click "SUBSCRIBE" in the menu. Enter your e-mail, and hit "SUBMIT." You will receive a confirmation e-mail. You should follow the instructions in the e-mail.

Social Media

As you look for library jobs, don't forget about social media. LinkedIn, Twitter, and even library-related blogs can be good tools to help during your job search.

LinkedIn is a professional networking tool that you can use to get connected to other professionals in the library community. You can also use it to assist with your job search and develop your professional network.

1. Create a free LinkedIn account, and make sure to upload relevant experience and skills, employment, volunteer work, etc.
2. Connect with current or former professors and classmates, library staff, former and current coworkers and supervisors, and other potential recommenders. Ask those who are knowledgeable of your skills and abilities to write recommendations to post on your LinkedIn profile.
3. Search for and join groups related to your career goals. "LIS Career Options" and "Library Workers Job Search and Careers" are two LinkedIn groups specifically dedicated to the job search for library professionals. Joining these groups or similar LinkedIn groups may help improve your odds of gaining employment through successful advice from group members, learning about an actual vacancy through the group, or increasing your network of connections on LinkedIn. "Information Science & LIS" and "Library and Information Technicians" are two LinkedIn groups for library professionals. Joining these groups can help you learn more about the library field and indicate to recruiters that you are actively trying to be involved in the library field (see figure 2.5).
4. Set up your career interests. You can do this by clicking on the jobs icon and then clicking on "CAREER INTERESTS." You can provide a note to recruiters, list specific job titles you are interested in, and identify your preferred locations, type of work (full-time, part-time, contract, etc.) you prefer, preferred industries, and even ideal size for an employer (see figure 2.6).
5. Let recruiters know you are interested in employment opportunities. You do this with the simple toggle of a digital button from "NO" to "YES." You can find the button by clicking on "CAREER INTERESTS" under "JOBS" (see figure 2.6).
6. Download and use the LinkedIn Job Search app to keep track of your viewed, saved, and applied positions. You can also search for jobs from this app. After typing a keyword in the search

box, you can filter the results based on relevance, location, date posted, company, job function, industry, and experience level.

Twitter allows users to follow and comment on everything from entertainment to politics, and job searching is no exception. Tweeters like Trending Librarian Jobs (@TrendingLibJobs) and ALA JobLIST Library & LIS Jobs (@ALA_JobLIST), and INALJ (Naomi House) (@NaomiINALJ) are among those that you should be following if you are looking for a library or library-related job. You can find academic library jobs on Trending Librarian Jobs. You can find jobs from ALA's job list promoted on ALA JobLIST Library & LIS Jobs. You can find jobs and other library-related tweets on INALJ. You can also choose to follow groups like the Amigos Library Svcs (@AmigosLibServ), a not-for-profit, membership base that services libraries, or your state library association to see even more job announcements.

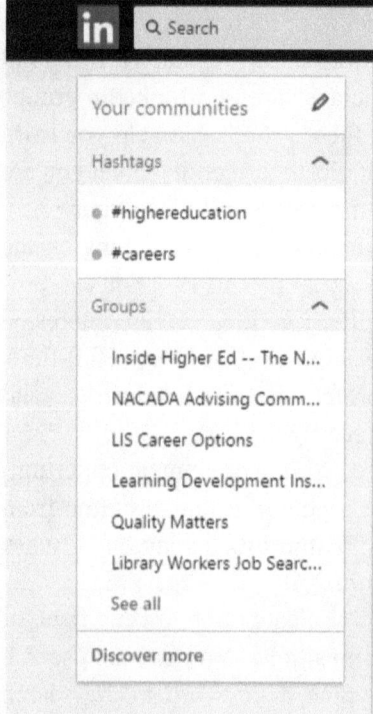

Fig. 2.5. You can click on "Discover More" to add additional groups to your LinkedIn profile.
LinkedIn, screenshot

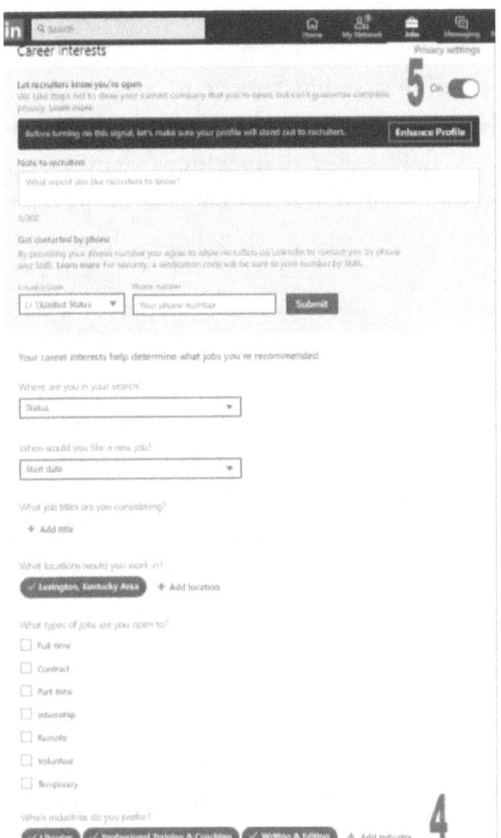

Fig. 2.6. This is a screenshot of the career interests section. Here you can define your career interests and let potential employers know whether you are actively looking.
LinkedIn, screenshot

Since it may be hard to know who to connect with on LinkedIn or follow on Twitter, you can also search for particular hashtags to broaden your scope when looking for a job. Some popular hashtags that hiring libraries and library-related organizations include on their posts and tweets include #libjobs, #lisjobs, #libraryjobs, and #libraryjob.

Library, library-related, and librarian blogs are another good source of information on your job search. *NASIG Jobs Blog* (https://nasigjobs.wordpress.com), *NH Library Jobline* (http://nhlibraryjobline.blogspot.com), *INALJ* (http://inalj.com), and the jobs page at *MLA Medical Library Association* (https://www.mlanet.org/jobs) are library and library-related sites that list current job openings for their target audience. LibGig's career blog (https://www.libgig.com/blog/) and *Library Career People* (https://librarycareerpeople.com) are popular blogs that provide a variety of career advice for your job search. *Mr. Library Dude* (https://mrlibrarydude.wordpress.com) and *Letters to a Young Librarian* (http://letterstoayounglibrarian.blogspot.com) are examples of librarian blogs that write about working in libraries and current issues and trends in the library field and that sometimes share career advice. *Hiring Librarians* (https://hiringlibrarians.com) is an inactive (but still available) library blog that houses an abundance of information related to hiring in libraries.

Search Engines

A final online tool to consider during your job search would be non-library-specific job-search engines. Job-search engines work by searching employer sites, job boards, and other websites for the latest job postings. These specialized search engines provide you many other benefits (e.g., saving résumés, jobs searches, etc.) beyond a basic searching feature. The major disadvantage to these general job-search engines is that you may see limited library jobs posted. However, you may find unique library-related organizations and jobs to add to your job-search process.

Indeed job-search website is free to job applicants and is a "pay-for-performance recruitment advertising network" that grants access to jobs posted on company websites and job boards. Indeed is used by over two hundred million users in over sixty countries.[14] You can use Indeed through its Web portal, mobile app, or e-mail. You can search by job title, keywords, or company and by city, state, and zip-code. Then after searching you can filter by date, type of job, or experience level. You can also sign up for e-mail updates based on your search, and Indeed gives you the option to create a résumé.

SimplyHired has free options for both the applicant and employer. SimplyHired posts jobs to Indeed and over one hundred other job sites, like CareerBliss, Jobster, StartWire, GetHired, and JobTarget, among others.[15] You can browse by type of job, company, city, or salary. You can search by job title, skills, or company and by city and state. You can filter your search by type of job, relevance, date added, or distance.

LinkUp searches the Web to collect job openings from employer websites to simplify your job search. You can search by job title, company, or keywords and by city, state, or zip. You can sort/filter by relevance (best match/most recent) or posting date. You apply directly through the employer's website not LinkUp. You can sign up for e-mail alerts following your search. When you create an account you can save jobs to apply for later. You can even save your search history to access later.

Monster identifies as a "global online employment solution" for job seekers and employers and boasts that 2,800 jobs are viewed on their site every minute.[16] You can search by keyword or title and location. You can filter further by radius, company, job status, cities nearby, and date. You can quickly access previous searches or set up a job alert to keep you posted on new positions as they are posted. You can also save jobs, e-mail jobs, and apply from the Monster website.

Personal Connections

In addition to online tools, you should definitely consider your interpersonal network and personal connections as additional avenues to find employment. Your interpersonal network is more than just your family and friends. It is built from connections you make in school, work, volunteer opportunities, and more. These connections can be used to learn about official job openings or connect you to others in the field.

School

The classroom is not just a good way to learn about being a librarian. It is also a great place to connect with persons interested in and practicing in the library industry. Through homework assignments, group work, guest speakers, practicums or internships, faculty, and other opportunities in the classroom you can develop some exceptional connections you may not achieve otherwise.

1. *Homework assignments.* You may complete a number of assignments throughout your library and information science education that result in connections you may be able to use later to help find a job. For example, a project that requires you to complete an

extensive library-profile including a librarian profile may lead to potential library connections. While this assignment and similar assignments may only provide limited interaction with the library profession, it is definitely an opportunity for you to inquire about connecting with them through social media like LinkedIn or asking if you can reach out when you begin your job search.
2. *Group work.* Through group work you can bond with your classmates. While that may not seem extremely valuable during the class, it can become extremely important after graduation. Through strong connections with classmates you may have an instant national or international network as you all start working in libraries across the globe. You should keep the names of classmates regardless of how close you get to them. You can reach out to your former classmates as potential collaborators in your job search (e.g., share your name with the hiring supervisor at their home library) or professional-development opportunities (e.g., conference presentations, papers, etc.).
3. *Guest speakers.* You should record information about any guest speakers you have in class. You should record their names, places of employment, topics of presentation, and the class they visited to use as a reminder of how your paths crossed. It would be appropriate to reach out to guest speakers about jobs in their library or library-related organization if you can remind them how you interacted with them.
4. *Practicums or internshisp.* Many library and information science programs require a practicum or internship as part of the degree requirements. Practicums and internships give you the opportunity to meet and interact with a number of library professionals at different levels in the organization. You should ask as many of your cointerns, supervisors, and other library staff as possible if you can connect with them through social-media services like LinkedIn or take their contact information for reaching out once you graduate. While some of these individuals may not feel comfortable being a reference, they may still be able to direct you to open positions once you graduate.
5. *Faculty.* Faculty offer another important connection in the classroom. If you received a good grade in the class and completed

memorable assignments then it may be appropriate to use them as a reference. Make sure you record information about the class(es) you took with the faculty member and some of your most successful assignments. Be sure to get the faculty member's permission before using them as a reference. You can also incorporate faculty as part of your job search by determining their connections in the library and information industry. Many faculty have connections outside of academia. They may be able to connect you to decision makers in many other libraries and library-related organizations they have interacted with through their research and/or other professional commitments.

Work and Volunteer Opportunities

You should be aware of connections you make through work and volunteer opportunities. These connections could include supervisors, coworkers, fellow volunteers, customers/clients or participants, vendors, and competitors. Keep a list of the contacts you meet, how you met (interacted with them), where they work, any contact information you are able to secure, and any other details you feel are important.

Alumni Network

The alumni network is a way to connect with other graduates from your school. These connections can be important in the job search. While you may not know everyone in your school alumni network, referencing your school name in your application materials may improve the likelihood your application materials will be considered if the school is a top library school or if the hiring officials have any connections to the school.

Professional Connections

Many professional associations host regional, statewide, national, and/or international conferences and build in multiple opportunities for networking. If you are attending a professional conference, go the extra step and attend any networking opportunities presented. Typically

> If you do not have business cards through your employer, you can use services like Vistaprint, Office Depot, or even your own personal printer to print your own cards. Just make sure if you print your own cards that you use your own personal contact information. Do not use logos of your school or employer without permission.

networking events include an opening or closing reception, sign-ups for group dinners or tours, interactive workshops, etc. You should participate in as many of these opportunities as possible, take notes (mental or written), and collect and distribute business cards.

Once the conference has ended reach out via e-mail or through social media to each person you met during the conference. If you are actively looking for employment, you might use this outreach to also inquire about a position in their library or library-related organization. Below are example e-mails or social-media requests you can customize and send if you are actively seeking employment.

EXAMPLE 1

Dear _____,
It was nice to meet you at the ALA mixer on January 14. As a soon-to-be graduate, I will be looking for employment soon. Would you happen to have a few minutes to meet with me to discuss possible openings within your library?
Sincerely,

_____

EXAMPLE 2

Dear _____,
It was nice to meet you at the YALSA mixer on January 14. I am very interested in being a teen librarian. Would you have a few minutes when I could call to ask you some questions about your position?
Sincerely,

_____

If you are not quite ready for a job, still reach out. Below is an example e-mail or social-media request you can customize and send if you are not actively seeking employment but want to build your professional network.

EXAMPLE 3

Dear _____,
It was nice to meet you at the ALA mixer on January 15. Would you please add me to your LinkedIn network? I am trying to expand my network of library and information science professionals, and I believe you would be a great addition to that network.
Sincerely,

_____

WHAT TO LOOK FOR

Determining your search terminology and search parameters before you start your search can make your search more productive.

Search Terminology

Knowing where to look for a job is only the first step. You also need to know what terminology to search. Using the appropriate terminology can yield better results. This section will review the most efficient terminology to use in your search.

The most obvious way to conduct a job search is to type in the job title. For example, if you want to be a children's librarian, then searching for "children's librarian" will likely deliver open positions available with that title. If you want to work at the information or reference desk, you can search for "reference librarian."

However, if you want to expand your search beyond mere job titles, you can search for other more general keywords. Many search engines and job boards allow you to enter keywords that may appear anywhere in the job posting. Using this option, you can search for positions requiring certain skills, requiring a particular education level, or expanding or narrowing your results.

Skills

You can identify key skills to include in your search in several different ways.

1. Look through current (or recent) library and library-related publications and websites. For example, in 2016 the *Library Journal* shared eleven new skills academic and public library directors identified as most significant for tomorrow's librarians.
2. Reach out to placement agencies or library schools to help identify key skills. LAC Group and the University of Southern California's Marshall Business School both identified key skills for those interested in working in libraries.
3. Review multiple job descriptions for your preferred type of library or library-related position. Then identify those skills most often listed, paying particular attention to those that seem most unique to that type of position.

You can use this newly created list in your search. Avoid generic skills that may also be key to positions unrelated to libraries. For example, technology skills were generically identified by the *Library Journal*, USC's Marshall Business School, and LAC Group, but technology skills are significant for many other positions, too. If you search generically for technology you will likely not receive many library-related positions. However, you can easily make your search more library-focused by identifying specific library technologies (e.g., integrated

> The *Library Journal* identified advocacy/politics, collaboration, communication/people skills, creativity/innovation, critical thinking, data analysis, flexibility, leadership, marketing, project management, and technological expertise as key skills librarians will need in the next twenty years.[17] USC's Marshall Business School provides a similar but shorter list for library students: be an information resource, be tech savvy, have multitasking and management skills, be an advocate, and have a sense of humor.[18] While there is no question these skills will be significant, few of these skills are unique to libraries. LAC Group on the other hand suggests much more specific skills that would be distinctive to libraries: information curation, in-depth and high-value research, digital preservation, mobile environment, and collaboration, coaching, and facilitation.[19]

library system, OPAC, online databases, etc.) or technology-related skills mentioned in the job announcement.

No matter what method or combination of methods you use to identify key skills for different library or library-related positions, you need to also consider your own top applicable skills for your keyword search. You can do this by conducting an inventory of your experience, education, and skills.

To conduct an inventory of your experience, education, and skills you should consider each of the following.

- *Review your previous employment and volunteer experience.* Try to identify key skills you used, knowledge gained or shared, etc. For example, if you worked as a receptionist in a doctor's office while in school, you likely gained skills in customer service and data entry, among other skills. You likely gained knowledge of office procedures, medical terminology, and specific softwares as well.
- *Consider any coursework you completed.* What topics were covered? What types of projects did you complete? What specific library processes or technologies did you learn about? For example, if you had to find and complete a grant application in one or more classes (even if you did not submit these for consideration) you likely further developed your research and writing skills.

Required Education

Another good way to search for jobs is by searching for positions that require a certain educational requirement. For example, if you are completing your master's in library science, searching for jobs that request a master's in library science for the educational requirement may allow you to expand your results to positions you may not already know. For example, a search on jobs in LinkedIn for "master's in library science" on September 21, 2018, resulted in 234 results worldwide. Included among the many library positions was an advertisement for a content designer for EBSCO Information Services and a media-monitoring specialist for Novartis Knowledge Center.[20]

Search Parameters

No matter which search technique or search terminology you use, you can restrict your search further by defining your search parameters. Some common search parameters include location, salary, educational requirements, and experience level.

Some job boards and search engines will let you filter automatically by certain parameters (see examples earlier in this chapter). However, even if the search engine will not allow filtering based on the additional criteria, you can restrict your applications manually by keeping the same filters in mind.

By defining your geographical preference in a job search you can restrict your results further. For example, you may be restricted geographically based on your family obligations, living arrangements, or another criteria. By adding this criteria you can make your job searching process more effective by focusing only on those positions that meet your limitations.

Another restrictive criterion can be salary. If you know that you cannot work for less than $32,000 a year, then you should not apply for positions that list a salary below that number. Similarly if you are a recent graduate you may remove positions that pay six figures unless the location has a higher standard of living or you hone the unique skills required. It makes sense to focus on positions within your own personal salary requirements and your experience.

Two other parameters that can help filter your results are educational requirements and experience requirements. By eliminating positions that require substantially more or less education or experience than you possess, you can make your job search more efficient.

WHEN TO LOOK

Timing sometimes plays a very significant role in securing a job. You should consider three timing aspects as you embark on your job search. First, you need to determine if you are ready to accept a position if offered. Second, you should determine when your choice library or library-related employer(s) typically post and fill positions. Third, you should consider the length of the hiring process.

> Personal obligations might include family vacations and medical procedures, among other things. Professional obligations might include a publication deadline, significant event (e.g., awards ceremony, summer advising program, etc.), funding/grant deadline, or other things covered by you in your current position. It is important to consider both personal and professional obligations to ensure that if you are offered a position you would be able to accept in a reasonable time. If the obligations would prevent you from accepting a position, you should wait to begin your job search.

When determining whether or not you are ready to apply for and accept a position, there are multiple considerations. Are you still in school? If so, when will you finish your degree program? Do you want to be employed immediately following school, or do you plan to take some time off? If you are not in school, are there other personal or professional obligations you have that may not make now the best time to apply?

Next, you need to determine when the library or library-related organization does its hiring. Libraries or library-related organizations may elect to hire at different times, but funding often dictates when a library or library-related organization fills a position. Libraries or library-related organizations may hire immediately following a vacancy or after a new position is approved/funded, or they may wait until a new budget year begins. Since there is no standard time when a library or library-related organization will hire, it is crucial for you to use the tools and techniques presented in this chapter to make sure you find out about different positions when they open.

Finally, how long does the hiring process take? Knowing that you are graduating in May does not mean you should start your job search in May. Many libraries and library-related organizations need weeks or even months to process applications, conduct interviews, make offers, complete required personnel documentation, etc. You should factor in the length of the hiring process into your plans. This means that if you want to start working in June you may want to start your job search no later than April. This may be challenging if you are still trying to complete coursework, but an early search means more time to find the best position for you.

NOTES

1. Bureau of Labor Statistics, "Job Openings and Labor Turnover Summary," *Economic News Release*, United States Department of Labor, accessed April 12, 2018, https://www.bls.gov/news.release/jolts.nr0.htm.

2. Bureau of Labor Statistics, "Librarians," *Occupational Outlook Handbook*, U.S. Department of Labor, last modified July 2, 2018, https://www.bls.gov/ooh/education-training-and-library/librarians.htm.

3. Richard Hernandez, "Online Job Search: The New Normal," Bureau of Labor Statistics, February 2017, https://www.bls.gov/opub/mlr/2017/beyond-bls/online-job-search-the-new-normal.htm.

4. AIM Library & Information Staffing, "About AIM," accessed June 24, 2018, https://www.aimusa.com/mission.php.

5. AIM Library & Information Staffing, "Application Form," accessed June 24, 2018, https://www.aimusa.com/app.php.

6. DHI Group, "We Are Specialized!" accessed April 12, 2018, https://www.dhigroupinc.com/home-page/default.aspx.

7. Robert Half International, "Employers: Simplify Your Search for Top Tech Talent," Work With Us: Our Services: Technology and IT, accessed September 20, 2018, https://www.roberthalf.com/work-with-us/our-services/technology#employers.

8. Robert Half International, "Job Seekers: How We Help You Find an IT Job—Fast," Work With Us: Our Services: Technology and IT, accessed September 20, 2018, https://www.roberthalf.com/work-with-us/our-services/technology#jobseekers.

9. San José State University, School of Information, "Benefits to Using Placement Agencies," College of Health and Human Services, accessed June 24, 2018, http://ischool.sjsu.edu/career-development/job-search-and-agencies/placement-agencies/benefits-using-placement-agencies.

10. Jefferson County Public Schools, "Library Media Specialist," accessed September 21, 2018, https://www.applitrack.com/jefferson/onlineapp/default.aspx?AppliTrackPostingSearch=location:%22HITE+ELEMENTARY%22 (link no longer active).

11. CareerBuilder, "About CareerBuilder," accessed April 11, 2018, https://hiring.careerbuilder.com/company/overview?_ga=2.114826119.125216564.1523526407-124352660.1467671469.

12. ZipRecruiter, "About," accessed April 12, 2018, https://www.ziprecruiter.com/about.

13. Glassdoor, "About Us," accessed April 9, 2018, https://www.glassdoor.com/about/index_input.htm.

14. Indeed, "About Indeed," accessed April 11, 2018, https://www.indeed.com/about.

15. SimplyHired, "Post Jobs Free," accessed April 12, 2018, https://www.simplyhired.com/post-jobs-free.

16. Monster, "About Monster Worldwide," accessed April 12, 2018, https://www.monster.com/about/.

17. Meredith Schwartz, "Top Skills for Tomorrow's Librarians: Careers 2016," *Library Journal*, March 9, 2016, https://www.libraryjournal.com/?detailStory=top-skills-for-tomorrows-librarians-careers-2016.

18. University of Southern California, Marshall School of Business, "Skills Today's Library Science Students Need for Career Success," *MMLIS Blog*, accessed September 21, 2018, https://librarysciencedegree.usc.edu/blog/skills-todays-library-science-students-need-for-career-success/.

19. LAC Group, "Top Five Skills Required for Librarians," August 6, 2016, https://lac-group.com/top-five-skills-required-for-librarians-today-tomorrow/.

20. LinkedIn, "380 Masters in Library Science Jobs, Careers in Worldwide," Jobs, accessed September 21, 2018, https://www.linkedin.com/jobs/search/?keywords=masters%20in%20library%20science&location=Worldwide&locationId=OTHERS.worldwide&start=125; the particular search results specified above are no longer found at this link.

BIBLIOGRAPHY

AIM Library & Information Staffing. "About Aim." Accessed June 24, 2018. https://www.aimusa.com/mission.php.

———. "Application Form." Accessed June 24, 2018. https://www.aimusa.com/app.php.

Bureau of Labor Statistics. "Job Openings and Labor Turnover Summary." Economic News Release. United States Department of Labor. Accessed April 12, 2018. https://www.bls.gov/news.release/jolts.nr0.htm.

———. "Librarians." *Occupational Outlook Handbook*. United States Department of Labor. Last modified July 2, 2018. https://www.bls.gov/ooh/education-training-and-library/librarians.htm.

CareerBuilder. "About CareerBuilder." Accessed April 11, 2018. https://hiring.careerbuilder.com/company/overview?_ga=2.114826119.125216564.1523526407-124352660.1467671469.

DHI Group. "We Are Specialized!" Accessed April 12, 2018. https://www.dhigroupinc.com/home-page/default.aspx.

Glassdoor. "About Us." Accessed April 9, 2018. https://www.glassdoor.com/about/index_input.htm.

Hernandez, Richard. "Online Job Search: The New Normal." Bureau of Labor Statistics. February 2017. https://www.bls.gov/opub/mlr/2017/beyond-bls/online-job-search-the-new-normal.htm.

Indeed. "About Indeed." Accessed April 11, 2018. https://www.indeed.com/about.

Jefferson County Public Schools. "Library Media Specialist." Accessed September 21, 2018. https://www.applitrack.com/jefferson/onlineapp/default.aspx?AppliTrackPostingSearch=location:%22HITE+ELEMENTARY%22.

LAC Group. "Top Five Skills Required for Librarians." August 6, 2016. https://lac-group.com/top-five-skills-required-for-librarians-today-tomorrow/.

LinkedIn. "380 Masters in Library Science Jobs, Careers in Worldwide." Jobs. Accessed September 21, 2018. https://www.linkedin.com/jobs/search/?keywords=masters%20in%20library%20science&location=Worldwide&locationId=OTHERS.worldwide&start=125.

Monster. "About Monster Worldwide." Accessed April 12, 2018. https://www.monster.com/about/.

Robert Half International. "Employers: Simplify Your Search for Top Tech Talent." Work With Us: Our Services: Technology and IT. Accessed September 20, 2018. https://www.roberthalf.com/work-with-us/our-services/technology#employers.

———. "Job Seekers: How We Help You Find an IT Job—Fast." Work With Us: Our Services: Technology and IT. Accessed September 20, 2018. https://www.roberthalf.com/work-with-us/our-services/technology#jobseekers.

San José State University, School of Information. "Benefits to Using Placement Agencies." College of Health and Human Services. Accessed June 24, 2018. http://ischool.sjsu.edu/career-development/job-search-and-agencies/placement-agencies/benefits-using-placement-agencies.

Schwartz, Meredith. "Top Skills for Tomorrow's Librarians: Careers 2016." *Library Journal*. March 9, 2016. https://www.libraryjournal.com/?detailStory=top-skills-for-tomorrows-librarians-careers-2016.

SimplyHired. "Post Jobs Free." Accessed April 12, 2018. https://www.simplyhired.com/post-jobs-free.

University of Southern California, Marshall School of Business. "Skills Today's Library Science Students Need for Career Success." *MMLIS Blog*. Accessed September 21, 2018. https://librarysciencedegree.usc.edu/blog/skills-todays-library-science-students-need-for-career-success/.

ZipRecruiter. "About." Accessed April 12, 2018. https://www.ziprecruiter.com/about.

CHAPTER 3

Applying for Jobs

Applying for and securing a job can be a complex, time-consuming task. This chapter will review the application process by first examining job descriptions and then describing different application materials and discussing how to manage applications.

UNDERSTANDING THE JOB DESCRIPTION

The amount of detail shared in a job description can vary by position and employer. Regardless of the amount of detail, you can use job descriptions to learn about the position, the library or library-related organization, and how to tailor application materials.

Components of a Job Description

There is no standard job-description format for library and library-related jobs; however, there are certain components that can be found in most job descriptions. Recognizing these components and knowing how to use them to your advantage is a very important part of the application process.

Many, but not all, job descriptions will include the name of the library or library-related organization. This information can be very helpful to you as an applicant. For example, if a job description includes the name, you can use this to learn more about the library or library-related organization. You can visit the library's website to learn more about its mission and purpose, services and programming, staff, etc. For library-related organizations you may also be able to do a search on a website like Glassdoor[1] to learn more about the working conditions. You may be able to learn more about a public library as an employer and community partner by contacting the Better Business Bureau[2] or the area chamber of commerce to see if there have been any reports by community members. You can conduct a Google search or a search on social media to see what employees and consumers have to say about the library or library-related organization.

Some libraries or library-related organizations provide a contact name, e-mail, and/or phone number for questions. This information can be useful in the application process. For example, a small to midsized library may list the library director as the contact. Larger libraries may list the director, the department manager, or a human resources representative. No matter the title or department of the person listed, you should address your application materials to that particular person, even if you know they are not the final decision maker. If you know nothing about the contact listed, you may be able to learn more about your potential supervisor or coworker by searching digital records on Google or finding or connecting with them through social media. It is very likely a potential employer might do the same with you.

If the job description only provides an e-mail address or phone number (no contact or organization name), you may be able to search that information on Google to find out more about who is behind the job posting. You could also send an e-mail or call the phone number, but you should make sure you have an idea of what to ask before doing this.

In addition to the organization name and contact information, the New Mexico State Library identifies six other key components to a library job description: position title and general summary, essential job duties or functions, nonessential duties, supervisory authority, special working conditions, and minimum qualifications.[3] You can learn valuable information from each of these components.

Position Title and General Summary

The position title and general summary can provide insights into a position. For example, if the word "supervisor" is in the position title, the likelihood that you would have to supervise someone would be

> Here is an example of a general summary for a sales engineer position posted by The Library Corporation (TLC):
>
> In the Sales Engineer position, the successful candidate will work directly with the CARL•X Strategic Account Consultants to deliver engaging and informative product presentations, assist with responses formal Requests for Proposal (RFP) and Requests for Information (RFI) in the Public Library market, and maintain proficiency in their assigned products' capabilities, usage, and configuration.[4]
>
> Through this general summary, applicants can learn briefly about the product(s), audience(s), and tasks that are a part of the position, using this information to identify key elements to incorporate into application materials. For example, applicants would want to be sure to include in their cover letter and résumé any experience they have using the CARL•X library automation system. Similarly, applicants experienced in working in a public library would certainly want to include mention of it, since this is the clientele for the product.

high. However, if the word "manager" is used in the position title, it is unclear through just the position title whether it includes supervising others. This is where the general summary can provide clarity.

The general summary is typically found at the beginning of the job description and provides a broad overview of the position. The general summary provides a quick reference you can use to gauge your interest in the position.

Sometimes a job may be identified by more than one position title in the description and/or general summary. You may see this typically in larger organizations where there might be multiple positions of the same type. For example, the University of South Carolina's University Libraries posted an opening for a position on September 6, 2018.[5] The internal title was listed as event coordinator, but the classification title (for university human resources' purposes) was program coordinator I.[6]

When you are applying for a job, it is important to understand the significance and difference in the titles and which to refer to in your application materials. The classification title is typically needed for personnel purposes and legal purposes. The internal title (also referred to as the "working title" at some organizations) is typically more representative of the actual duties and used by employees and the public. In your cover letter you should refer to the position by the internal title or the title referenced the most in the description.

Essential Job Duties or Functions

The essential job duties or functions tend to be the largest part of a job description. The duties or functions section provides a detailed description of daily, weekly, monthly, and annual activities, projects, and events that may fall within the purview of the position. Keep in mind that in most cases the list of duties will not be exhaustive but should be summative of the major responsibilities of the position. Many times identifying and focusing on key activities, projects, or events found in the job description in your application materials may increase your odds of landing an interview.

Nonessential Duties

Some job descriptions include extra duties that may not be essential. When applying for a job it is important to identify the nonessential to avoid focusing on the wrong duties in your application materials. For example, Crown College lists both essential functions and optional duties for its director of library and media services. If applying for this position,

> The Lincoln County Library System in Wyoming posted a branch manager position for its Star Valley branch on October 2, 2018. In that description the library groups the essential duties into eight primary categories. Within each category, the library identifies specific duties. In such an instance, you should try to align your application materials with specific duties under each area. For example, under "Programs and Services" the library specifies as example duties that the branch manager "arranges for displays, exhibits, and special programs" and is "responsible for collection development for the branch, including selection and weeding."[7] If you have related experience in an area specified in the job posting, you need to include it on your résumé or curriculum vitae (CV), and if the experience is significant, you may want to include it in your cover letter.

you should make sure you focus on those items in the essential-functions section of the job description, not those additional duties. While it may be enticing to have the opportunity to teach one course (optional duties), it is more significant that you can demonstrate your abilities to "provide vision and direction for strategic planning" and "assess library services and resources in accordance with accreditation standards (essential duties)."[8]

Supervisory Authority

If the job title contains the word "supervisor," or, likewise, if the description identifies a number of persons you would supervise in the advertised role, it is a strong indicator that the position is a supervisory role. This may be highlighted in a stand-alone section title, or the supervisor reference may be found in the general description or the essential job duties and functions. If the position appears to require supervision experience, make sure to highlight applicable supervisory experience in your application materials.

Special Working Conditions

Some job descriptions will include details about the working conditions. This is especially true if travel or driving is an essential part of the job. For example, most outreach or bookmobile positions would mention any requirements for driving and/or traveling to locations throughout the community. While this is important for you to know, it is not essential for you to provide details about your driving record in your résumé or cover letter. You can certainly include details from previous travel- or outreach-based positions to demonstrate your related experience and interest in a similar position, but it is not necessary to explicitly state you have a driver's license. You can provide that information on the official application or at a later time if asked.

Minimum Qualifications

Most job descriptions list the minimum requirements (sometimes referred to as "required qualifications") accepted by the organization. You should read over these requirements before applying for a position. You may not be considered if you do not meet the minimum requirements; however, sometimes exceptions are made. Minimum or required qualifications are usually quantified by number of years of experience and type of degree and qualified by type of experience and area of study.

The primary way employers restrict the applicant pool is by requiring a certain number of years of experience. You can determine whether or not you meet the number of years of experience by totaling your full-time experience in the desired field. Remember, part-time work experience may count toward your total years of experience, but you may need to convert it to its full-time equivalent. You should not count part-time employment the same as full-time employment when estimating your years of experience.

Employers will attempt to further restrict the applicant pool by specifying the type of degree applicants must hold (associate's, bachelor's, master's, doctorate). Each degree level indicates disciplined study at the collegiate level. Many employers request a degree to prove some level of mastery in a specific subject area.

Employers usually include desired types of experience and areas of study in the job descriptions. You can use this information to further evaluate whether you should apply for the position. Typically if a position includes a required or preferred type of experience, you should

---

Here is an example of the minimum (required) qualifications for a metadata librarian I position advertised at EBSCO Information Services:

> Master in Library Science from ALA accredited program. Candidates who are currently enrolled in a Master's program and are within one semester of graduating will also be considered and are encouraged to apply.
>
> At least 1 year of experience in descriptive and subject cataloging and bibliographic record creation in MARC format.
>
> Professional knowledge of cataloging procedures and principles through 1–3 years' experience or equivalent coursework in descriptive and subject cataloging and bibliographic record creation in MARC format.[9]

Notice this particular position requires a master's in library science from an ALA-accredited program and a minimum of one year of experience with MARC-related cataloging. This primarily quantitative information establishes the minimum criteria EBSCO will consider of applicants.

expect to provide specific evidence (usually paid and full-time) in this area or a related area. For example, when the School of Information Sciences at the University of Illinois at Urbana–Champaign was hiring a senior lecturer, in the job description the school specifically requested "significant professional experience" in one or more designated areas, including adult and public services, collection development, reference and information services, and more.[10] In your application materials for such a position you should speak directly to those qualifications. If you have experience developing research guides or experience working in virtual reference you should include this information, along with your teaching experience, in your application materials, and if the number of research guides developed or hours of reference worked are significant, then you should include that information to further establish your knowledge of these reference functions.

When a posting specifies an area of study, it is expected you will have extensive knowledge on a certain topic. Sometimes experience can substitute for an area of study, but ideally the area of study will demonstrate significant theoretical, historical, or application-based study in a designated area. For example, many academic-librarian positions will specify that applicants have additional graduate study (e.g., a master's degree) in another subject area. Humanities librarians or liaisons to humanities departments in colleges and universities often require a secondary master's in a humanities area (e.g., English, history). When you have this additional accomplishment, be sure to include it on your résumé/CV, and, if it is a focus of the job description, you may even want to include this credential in your cover letter.

If minimum requirements are not listed, you should not assume this means there are no minimum requirements. It may be worth investigating more before you apply. You could contact the library or library-related organization, or you could review similar job postings or general job descriptions to see what minimum requirements are listed. The Maine State Library, the New Mexico State Library, and the Association for Information Science and Technology all have sample library and library-related job descriptions that may help you determine minimum requirements.[11]

Both the quantitative and qualitative requirements can help you determine whether or not you are qualified and reveal important information about the job, the organization, and its culture and people. However, understand that sometimes libraries or library-related organizations may consider additional education in place of required experience or vice versa even if not explicitly stated in the job description. For example, the University of Kentucky provides a link to equivalencies for many of its job descriptions.[12] As an applicant you can use this to determine if your combined education and experience can substitute for the minimum education or experience requirements.

Optional Information

Some job descriptions may include additional information you can use to further evaluate your interest in the position. Schedule/work hours, location information, and salary are examples of key optional information.

Some job descriptions include proposed working hours. Those hours can be important in determining whether you want to apply for a position or not. If you cannot work the hours listed, then it may not be worth your time to apply. If the description lists hours but says "after hours as needed" or only mentions that "hours vary," this may be an indication that there will be expectations beyond a regular workday. You need to decide if you are willing to work additional and/or altered hours. If you are not willing or able to work additional or altered hours, then this may be a reason not to apply for a position. If you are unsure, you could still apply and pose the hours question at the appropriate time during the application process.

Some job descriptions include detailed information about the city or town where the position reports or the service area it covers. This information can be especially useful if you are looking for employment in a different geographical location. It can also indicate that a library or library-related organization is open to accepting nonlocal candidates.

Some job descriptions specify the primary reporting location for the position. For example, if you are applying to be a school-media specialist for a school district, the position may be for a specific school in that district, or if it is a very small school district with limited funds the school-media specialist may be required to travel between school locations to provide library services to all students in the district.

Some job descriptions include salary ranges, and some do not. Those that provide salary help streamline the application process by prefiltering applications. When you are reviewing job descriptions you should consider any salary information in your decision to apply. If a salary listed is not within the range of what you are willing to accept, then that may be a strong reason not to apply. Most organizations do not go beyond the listed salary when filling a position.

Dissecting Language Used in a Job Description

Once you decide to apply for a position, you should look at the language used in the job description and try to incorporate similar keywords and/or concepts in your application materials. While this requires additional time, it demonstrates you made an effort to customize your application materials for the position and that you know what the expectations are for the position.

You can identify key action verbs, skills, or terminologies by reviewing the essential duties or functions, general summary, and even the qualifications section of the job description. Using as an example the sales engineer position posted at TLC mentioned earlier in this chapter, the key concepts that stand out are the CARL integrated library system (ILS), public library, product presentations, technical and presentation support, and RFP and bid requests. If you were applying for this position, it would be important to include specific reference to as many of these concepts as possible. For example, if you have experience specifically with CARL, you want to include that in your application materials. If you don't have specific experience with CARL but have experience with other ILS, you should highlight this ILS experience without identifying the specific system or identify all other systems you have used. What you want to avoid is sabotaging your own application by highlighting your lack of experience specifically in CARL.

Another key reason to customize your application materials is the increasing use of automated applicant-screening software. Automated application-screening software or services allow the library or library-related organization to restrict the number of applications seen by the hiring officials based on the inclusion of certain keywords, years of

> The University of Kentucky receives hundreds of applications for most of its positions. Through its automated application system, UK's human resources department is able to restrict the number of applications seen by the hiring library or department by asking a number of screening questions during the application submission. For example, in September 2018, Institutional Research and Advanced Analytics at UK was seeking applications for a senior data-management specialist. The first screening question they posed was "How man(y) years of paid, full-time employment experience do you have working with enterprise reporting tools?"[13] This question could be used to automatically determine whether or not applicants met the minimum requirements. Applicants were asked to select the response that most closely matched their experience in the field. If an applicant's answer did not meet the minimum acceptable qualification, then the application was not likely released to the hiring committee.

experience, etc. This is typically done through the use of screening questions required when an application is submitted.

APPLICATION MATERIALS

Two key application pieces are most often used when applying for a professional librarian or library-related position: the résumé, or CV, and a cover letter. This section will explain the purpose of each application piece (résumé, CV, and cover letter), review key formatting considerations for each application piece, introduce expected and optional content for each application piece, and end with a brief look at some other items a library or library-related organization may request as part of an application.

Purpose

Regardless of the type of position you are applying for, you will likely be asked to provide a résumé or CV and a cover letter. Each document serves a specific purpose in the application process.

A résumé is your chance to introduce the hiring team to your skills and qualifications that would benefit a potential employer. The primary purpose of this document is just that—to record and highlight certain key skills you possess, experiences you've had, awards you've earned, and education you've completed that make you a good candidate for a particular position. Résumés may be generic but are often more successful if the content is customized for the position you are seeking (see the "Expected and Optional Content" section for more details).

A CV is similar to a résumé in that it lists your skills, experience, awards, and other achievements but is often required for faculty positions. The key difference between a résumé and CV is that you should plan to include every applicable activity, award, etc., in your CV. Your CV should serve as a comprehensive view of your accomplishments instead of focusing on just those relevant to your current job search.

A cover letter is a companion piece to either your résumé or CV (see the description of the job you are applying for to determine which document the library or library-related organization requests). The purpose of the cover letter is to provide a more detailed explanation of how your qualifications match specific requirements (skills, education, etc.) provided in the position description. You should plan to customize your cover letter to each library or library-related position.

Formatting

Your résumé or CV and cover letter should represent you but also meet any specifications established by the hiring library or library-related organization as well as meet some generally accepted (and expected) formatting standards. Below is a list of some key elements you should consider when it comes to formatting your résumé or CV and your cover letter.

1. *Length.* The length of each application document may vary depending on your experience and qualifications, but all should be relatively short but detailed. You should keep your résumé between one and two pages. You should keep your cover letter to one page. Your CV, if you create one, would be the one exception: CVs are intended to include all of your experience and qualifications and so may continue for several pages. Typically a

long CV is seen as a positive in the hiring process, but lengthier résumés and cover letters are frowned upon.
2. *Consistent layout.* There are multiple elements that should be formatted similarly in both your résumé or CV and your cover letter:
   a. *Spacing.* When creating your résumé or CV and your cover letter, you need to use spacing appropriately. Poor spacing may make it difficult to meet page recommendations and may also make it more challenging for the hiring committee to evaluate your skills. In general (unless noted otherwise) you should plan to single space your application materials, with an extra line space between sections (in your résumé or CV) or between paragraphs (in your cover letter). If you are knowledgeable and comfortable with changing the spacing in your word-processing program, you may be able to adjust the spacing to a range between single and double spacing to better use white space and make your résumé, CV, or cover letter seem fuller (if short) or hold slightly more information.
   b. *Margins.* You may not automatically think about margins, since most word-processing programs use the standard one-inch margins, but margins can be very important in making your résumé, CV, and your cover letter look consistent.
   c. *Font.* You should plan to use a standard font that is easily legible. Sans serif fonts like Arial, Calibri, or Helvetica are good choices, because they work well both with application systems that search for keywords and with printing for search committees.
3. *Alignment.* You should align text in your résumé, CV, and cover letter so that the information appears uniform and easy to read. For your résumé or CV, this means placing dates on the same side, using tabs to space appropriately between different elements of an entry, etc. The author has included previous versions of her résumé and CV in appendix 2 to demonstrate some of the different ways you can align a résumé or CV.

   In your cover letter, all elements (except the header) need to be right-aligned. You should avoid indenting paragraphs unless requested by the library or library-related organization. The one

exception is the header, which if centered on your résumé or CV should also be centered on the cover letter.
4. *Uniform headers.* You should plan to use the same header information and style for all your application materials. This header should contain some basic information about you, including your name, mailing address, e-mail address, and phone number. If you choose to include other digital/interactive media (e.g., Facebook profile, Twitter handle, LinkedIn profile, etc.), you need to make sure you manage those accounts appropriately. This means monitoring what is tagged and/or shared with you and checking each account regularly. You may be better off omitting digital/interactive media unless the announcement specifies it be included.

Expected and Optional Content

When trying to determine what to include in your application materials, you should consider both what is expected to be included and what optional information you want to include. The section below will review expected and optional content for your résumé, CV, and cover letter.

Résumé

As stated previously, your résumé should be one to two pages in length and highlight at least your employment experience and education. You may wish to note any volunteer work, notable skills, and other significant details related to your employability. Do not include personal details like age, race, religion, gender, and sexual orientation. The only exception should be if your employment, volunteer work, and skills reflect that type of personal information. For example, if you teach a children's Sunday school class and you are applying to be a children's librarian, then your experience leading a group of children may be vital experience to include to help you get the job.

You should review your employment history, education, volunteer experience/community service, leadership roles, and awards/honors to begin. You can start by making a list of these things, but ultimately you will need to identify specific skills and experience associated with many of these. And while you should not list hobbies on a résumé, it might be helpful to consider skills you gain or continue to develop in your hobbies.

The information you collect may dictate what information you choose to include and how you organize that information. The three most common ways to organize a résumé are chronological, functional, or a combination of the two. No one organizational style is by default better than any other. You should consider your own accomplishments, the job description, and the library or library-related organization when selecting the most appropriate type of résumé to submit.

A *chronological résumé* is the most straightforward view of your qualifications. Very simply, a chronological approach means you provide your experience and qualifications in order of occurrence, with the most recent at the top. Most applicants use work experience and education as the two major headings. Some applicants may include additional sections for volunteer experience and for awards and honors, all with information listed chronologically, the most recent first.

In constructing your chronological résumé, you should include relevant, paid employment experience in the work-experience section. The information should be listed in the order it was attained, with the most recent first. You should include for each position at least the dates of employment (month/year), the name of the employer, the location (optional), the title of the position, and a description of the duties performed. The duties can be a bulleted list, a series of phrases or words separated by commas, or short sentences. Some applications also include an optional narrative description of each position held. The goal of the work-experience section is to provide a snapshot of your experience. Below is an example of a work-experience entry on one résumé.

EXAMPLE

Library Student Worker,
   Lexington Theological Seminary   May 2010–November 2010
Optional Narrative Description:
- Assisted patrons face-to-face and online with circulation and reference needs

- Conducted inventory and shelved books
- Updated and entered records for new periodical arrivals
- Utilized Millennium ILS and Microsoft Excel regularly

While this example is not the only way you can format your work-experience section, there are some important things you should note about this entry.

Notice each bulleted item starts with a past tense action verb. This is important for several different reasons:

1. You build consistency in your résumé by starting each detail with an action verb. You should avoid switching between beginning with subject or verb in your lists of experiences.
2. You define your participation in the process, product, event, etc.
3. You adhere to the résumé standard practice of using the past tense for previous positions held.[14]

You can use volunteer experience to build up your chronological résumé, especially when you lack paid experience or have gaps in your work history. However, volunteer experience should not be listed along with paid employment in a work-experience section. If you have significant volunteer experience or lack work experience, you may elect to combine your volunteer and work experience into one section simply titled "Experience." Otherwise you need to keep volunteer experience separate to avoid sending a potential employer false messages. The volunteer-experience section should include similar information as that found in the work-experience section: dates of service, the name of the organization, the title of the volunteer or other role you held, etc. You may elect to include a brief

> Some common words that may relate to your previous experience include "supervised," "developed," "created," "maintained," "managed," "coordinated," "edited," "analyzed," "delegated," "collected," and "solved." While this is a good start for action verbs, you should use a thesaurus or perform a search online for "action verbs for résumés" to expand your vocabulary. You should avoid repeating your action verbs when possible.

description of the organization and/or its purpose, but remember that the focus is to demonstrate the valuable skills and experience you gained through your volunteer experience. Below is an example of a volunteer-experience entry on a résumé.

EXAMPLE

Friends of Public Library, City, State   January 2019–present
Friends of Public Library is a group of library patrons who volunteer to promote the library and raise money through the annual friends' book sale.
- Assist with registration at annual summer-reading events
- Select and price books for the ongoing friends' book sale

This example is library-specific, but you may certainly include volunteer experiences outside of libraries if you deem them relevant. Similar to your work experience, you can highlight specific projects, events, or services that were part of your volunteer work. Any specific details should follow the same action verb format as with your work experience.

You should plan to include relevant awards or honors you received, because these highlight recognition you have received for hard work. The awards and honors can be personal or professional in nature but should only be listed if you believe they will distinguish you as a candidate and seem relevant to the position. In a chronological résumé, awards or honors should be listed by date received, with the most recent first. You should include the date received, the name of the award or honor, the sponsoring organization, and a brief description of the award (optional) and why you received it. Some examples of honors and awards may be scholarships, dean's list placement, or leadership awards. Awards and honors can be included as a separate section on the résumé or may be included within a specific section. Below are two different examples of how you can include awards and honors on a résumé.

EXAMPLE 1, WITH SEPARATE AWARDS SECTION

AWARDS
Graduate Assistantship,   August 2000–June 2001
  Western Kentucky University

EXAMPLE 2, WITHOUT SEPARATE AWARDS SECTION

EDUCATION
Master of Arts in Communication, Western Kentucky University   2001
Awarded graduate assistantship, August 2000–June 2001

You should include information regarding your education, especially when you possess or are completing the required education. You should include the name of the school, your dates of attendance or the date the degree was awarded, the type of degree you obtained, and the subject you studied. Optional information may include grade point average (GPA), specializations or minors, or specific courses completed. Below are two different examples of ways you could list your education on a résumé. Notice both are organized chronologically, with the most recent schooling first.

EXAMPLE 1

EDUCATION
June 2017–Aug. 2018	Graduate Certificate in Career Services, Western Kentucky University
June 2008–May 2010	Master of Science in Library Science, University of Kentucky
July 2000–Dec. 2001	Master of Arts in Communication, Western Kentucky University
Aug. 1995–Dec. 1998	Bachelor of Arts in Business Administration, Kentucky State University

EXAMPLE 2

EDUCATION
University of Kentucky, Lexington Master of Science in library science GPA	2010
Western Kentucky University, Bowling Green Master of Arts in communication One-year graduate assistantship GPA	2001
Kentucky State University, Frankfort	1998

Bachelor of Arts in business administration
Marketing specialization
GPA

A *functional résumé* may use similar information to what is found in a chronological résumé, but it is organized differently. You should focus on your skills and knowledge and less on where and when you gained those skills. In addition to skills and knowledge, you should also include work history and education. You can add awards and honors or volunteer work if you have substantial accomplishments in those areas. A functional résumé is a good option if you have gaps in your employment history or limited professional library or library-related experience.

The skills section is the distinguishing characteristic of a functional résumé. You should focus on two things in the skills section: First, consider your own experience. What skills have you gained through

---

Considering an embedded librarian position? Embedded librarians at most colleges and universities are required to work within the school's learning-management system (LMS). If you have already graduated or are attending an iSchool, you should have experience as a user in a learning-management system and should plan to include that in your functional résumé. However, since your experience is limited to that of a user, you may need to group this with other technology experience you have under a single Technology Experience header. Below is an example of a technology-skills entry on a functional résumé.

EXAMPLE

RELEVANT SKILLS
Technology Skills
- Participated in discussions, submitted assignments, and completed exams in Canvas learning-management system
- Created interactive presentations using Microsoft PowerPoint and Adobe Presenter
- Moderated group project using GroupMe App

Reading over any embedded-librarian job description you should be able to identify additional relevant skill sets you could add to your functional résumé.

your experience (work and volunteer) and your education? Second, consider the key skills outlined in the job description. How do those skills intersect with the skills you identified? Once you determine that intersection between your skills and those required by the position, you can use those to build the foundation for your skills section.

Each entry of the employment or work-history section of the functional résumé includes the name of your employer, the location (optional), the title of your position, and your dates of employment (month/year). You may choose to include a brief description of your duties, but this should be limited in scope. Typically there is no need to include details of the work performed, since you would include that information in the skills section. Below is one example of the work-history section in a functional résumé.

EXAMPLE

EMPLOYMENT
Lecturer, University of Kentucky,   Apr. 2014–Dec. 2016
    School of Information Science
Technology Manager,   Mar. 2012–Mar. 2014
    Scott County Public Library
Student Library Worker,   May 2010–Nov. 2010
    Lexington Theological Seminary

The education section should be included in a functional résumé even though you may include some of the skills, knowledge, or experience you gained in the skills section. You can list the education in a similar fashion as the employment. You do not have to provide any substantial detail unless you want to highlight GPA or other accomplishments.

EXAMPLE

EDUCATION
Master of Science in Library Science,   May 2010
    University of Kentucky
Master of Arts in Communication,   Dec. 2001
    Western Kentucky University
Bachelor of Arts in Business Administration,   Dec. 1998
    Kentucky State University

Since the focus of a functional résumé is on skills and experience it may be important to include any training you have completed in addition to education. You can include this in the same section as education and title it "Education and Training," or you can develop a separate section. You should make the decision based on the types of training you have completed. For example, if you completed Google for Education's Certified Trainer Program, then this could be easily added to your education section above since you can list the certification, company, and date received.

While not required, you could include any awards or volunteer experience on a functional résumé as well. You could include separate sections for these, or you could share these experiences and honors by indicating what valuable skills you gained as part of these experiences.

A *combination résumé* applies the strengths of both résumé types and typically works best for someone who may have a significant work history. You may consider using a combination résumé if you intend to highlight certain skills but also have significant work experience—inside or outside of the area in which you are seeking work.

One significant difference in the combination résumé is the inclusion of a brief statement about your skills, knowledge, and experience—often referred to as a professional profile, summary, or qualifications.[15] This statement can be written as a bulleted list or a series of short sentences or phrases. You can also include a skills or highlights section if it seems relevant.

EXAMPLE

PROFESSIONAL PROFILE
University faculty with over 5 years of teaching experience. Knowledgeable in Blackboard and Canvas learning-management systems, Zoom, and other online educational tools.

Combination résumés contain a work history similar to that of a chronological résumé. You should list each position chronologically, with the most recent first. You should include the dates of employment (month/year), the name of your employer, the location (optional), the title of your position, and a description of the duties you performed or the accomplishments you achieved. You can write the duties or accomplishments as a bulleted list, a series of phrases or words separated by commas, or short sentences. The duties should not be written in paragraph format unless requested by the employer. Remember, the goal here is to demonstrate how that position matches up to a significant skill required in the position you are seeking.

There are some variations possible in a combination résumé. One variation would be to group related positions together instead of merely listing them chronologically. For example, if you have held multiple jobs as a library clerk you can group these all together under the heading "Library Clerk Experience," even if the positions were years apart and you held other positions between them. If you are lacking on library experience but have significant customer-service experience, you can combine your previous retail, restaurant, or other customer-service experiences together under a section titled "Customer Service Experience." Then with each entry you can list the specific customer-service-related duties associated with that position. You can include another section called "Additional Experience" for other positions you have held if there is not another logical way to group those together.

You should also include an education section and consider adding an awards and honors section, if applicable, to your combination résumé. These sections should include the title of the degree or award, the school or issuing organization, and the date you earned it.

Curriculum Vitae (CV)

CVs include multiple sections and list items in those sections chronologically, with the most recent first. CVs are typically multiple pages, and yours will grow in length as your experience and accomplishments increase. See appendix 2 for an example of a CV.

Your CV should start with education. List your most recent education first, and include the name of the institution attended, the degree earned (e.g., PhD, MS, BA), the discipline or field of study, your GPA, dissertation or thesis information, and any other relevant information.

Most CVs start with education first. The sections that follow may vary in order depending on your achievements and may need to be reorganized depending on the focus of the position you are seeking. Those sections include awards, library experience, research (publications, presentations, etc.), teaching responsibilities, committee work, other professional experience, association membership, etc.

You should consider your own achievements and the job description/position when selecting the order of the remaining items on your CV. For example, if you have extensive teaching experience and you are applying for an instructional librarian position, then it may make sense to list your teaching experience next. If you are applying for a research or subject-area-expert position, then if you have conducted extensive research or published in that particular subject you may want to lead with research or publications after education.

If you have received scholarships, fellowships, grants, and other applicable awards, you may want to list these accomplishments near the beginning of your CV. These may help you distinguish yourself as a candidate, especially if the awards had large monetary figures attached. Awards should include the title of the award, the date granted, the granting body, the amount (if applicable) or type of award, and a brief description of the award.

Since you are likely applying for or working in an academic library if you are constructing a CV, you should plan to have a separate section devoted to library experience if applicable. You should include your job title, the name of the library, your dates of employment (month/year), the location (optional), and a description of your accomplishments or duties at that job.

Research is a crucial component for most academic librarians. Whether you are assisting other faculty with their research or conducting your own, you will likely be required to participate in research. You should include significant research projects you have contributed to or led in this section. This might include research projects or grant proposals, publications, presentations, etc. You can select how you want to organize this section. You should include the title, contributors, the funding organization, the amount of funding, the award or completion dates, etc., for research projects or grant proposals. You should include citations for any publications you wrote or on which you were listed as co-author. This might include white papers, dissertations, theses, articles, or books. You may also include the presentation title, the presenters, the conference title, the dates, etc., of any applicable presentations or research.

Not all library faculty have teaching responsibilities, but if you are applying to be an instructional librarian or have experience teaching college, you should plan to include this in your CV. Almost all college and university librarians must interact with students, so including any teaching experience you have can demonstrate your proficiency in working with students. You should include titles of any classes or workshops you taught or even contributed content to or moderated online. You should include the dates of instruction and the school or library affiliation during instruction. You may want to include the number and type of students.

Service on and off campus is an expectation for most faculty positions. You should keep a current and accurate list of your committee work. You can list your position (e.g., chair, member, coordinator), committee name, and dates of service.

Faculty sometimes have experience in areas outside of academia and libraries. If applicable, you should certainly include these types of positions on your CV. Be sure to include your title, the name of the organization, the dates of employment (month/year), and a brief description of duties and/or listing of accomplishments. The description can be a bulleted list, phrases separated by commas, or short sentences.

Noting your memberships in professional associations is an important way to demonstrate your knowledge of and participation in the library field. You should list all memberships (current and past) that are relevant to librarianship and otherwise demonstrate your commitment to professional development. This might include local, state, and national associations. You can find a list of many library and library-related associations in appendix 1. Other memberships you might consider listing include organizations such as Toastmasters, local job clubs, library friends associations, and community boards.

Cover Letter

A cover letter often accompanies a résumé or CV and provides a more detailed explanation of how your qualifications match the position description. You should customize your cover letter for each position. Despite the customization, all cover letters should include some essential elements. An example cover letter that led to a job interview is offered in appendix 3.

You should start your cover letter with the same header that you used in your résumé or CV and then include the standard elements found in a traditional business letter: the date, the receiver's contact information, and a salutation.

- *Date.* You should include the date of your application on the cover letter. Even though much of the application process is digitally time stamped at the time you apply, it is still important to include a date on your letter, as many organizations still distribute printed or digital copies of the application materials to those making the hiring decisions. The date reinforces to hiring officials that your materials are current and up-to-date. It confirms to hiring officials that your application was submitted at the appropriate time.
- *Recipient's address.* After the date, you should include the recipient's address. In some cases this address may be provided in the job posting. If so, then use this address. In many cases an address may not be included, but this should not stop you from finding and including the recipient's address. This is an opportunity to show your information-seeking skills—a valuable skill for most librarians and information professionals—and may indicate to the library or library-related employer your initiative and determination.
- *Salutation.* As with seeking out the recipient's address, if you can find the name of a hiring manager or decision maker you should include that name in the salutation. Again, if a personal contact is not provided in the job posting, identifying the most likely candidate to receive the letter can demonstrate important information-seeking skills. You may be able to determine the most likely candidate by visiting the library or library-related organization's website. From the website you will likely be able to determine whether or not there is a human resources department or a department manager for the area to which you are applying. If so, these are all good candidates for the salutation. If you cannot find an organizational chart or contact (and one is not listed in the

job description) then you may consider a generic salutation like "Dear hiring official" or "Dear search committee."

After the salutation, you should plan to write at least three paragraphs in your letter. Each paragraph or section serves a specific function. The first paragraph or introduction should identify the position, express your interest in the position, introduce your qualifications for the position, and indicate where you learned about the position. The next paragraph(s) should expand on your qualifications for the position. The final paragraph should include a summarizing statement to remind the reader(s) of your qualifications, mention your attached résumé or CV, reference the job title and hiring organization, request an interview, and supply your contact information.

Your introduction should start with a statement indicating your interest in the position. Be sure to identify the position by the designated title used in the job posting. You should also identify where you learned of the opening. This is important to human resources professionals monitoring employment resources. Also, if you learned of the position from an employee or personal connection, saying so can sometimes improve the likelihood you will be considered for the position. The last part of the opening paragraph needs to address your qualifications for the position and preview the body of the letter.

There are many ways you can construct each component in the introduction. Below is one example of an introduction used in an actual cover letter.

EXAMPLE

Since completing my Master of Science in library science (MSLS) in May 2010, I have been searching for full-time employment in a library in central Kentucky. With the availability of the technology manager position at the County Public Library, advertised on the library's website, I know I have found the full-time library position I have been seeking. As technology manager I can combine my interests in teaching and technology to build stronger information-seeking behaviors and information-literacy skills across County not only by helping patrons learn and understand new emerging technologies but also by helping the library successfully carry out its technology goals.

In the next paragraph(s) you should detail how your experience and/or education align with specific requirements of the position. It is important in this section to provide detailed examples and/or specific information related to the position. This section should not be generic and reused for all applications. It should be specific for the current application. For example, if you are applying for a job as a library branch manager, be sure to include specific information about your supervisory and/or management skills even if they are not in libraries. You may quantify your supervisory experience by sharing how long or how many people you have supervised. You may try to qualify your experience by sharing a brief story of how you delegated to others under your supervision, resolved a conflict between employees, or even calmed an irrational patron.

Your closing should come as one concise paragraph that summarizes your qualifications, mentions your résumé or CV, reminds the hiring professionals what position you are seeking, and asks for the interview. The summarizing statement is similar to that found in the introduction. Don't forget to mention the résumé or CV and the name of the position you are seeking. Finally, in the closing statement you should ask

Below is an example actually used in securing a library job. The writer identified technology experience as one of the key skills found in the description and wrote the following paragraph to highlight her own technology experience.

EXAMPLE

I have technology experience beyond course development. I have maintained three websites and one repository of information. Currently I use Dreamweaver to post new items on the institute's website. I maintained the Georgetown News-Graphic website using a content-management system. I set up interactive pages with surveys and contests, designed and posted interactive Internet ads, approved comments about news stories, administered the e-mail-alerts program, posted classified ads and special sections from the paper on the website, and administered special projects such as the Letters to Santa and the Letters to Troops.

for the interview (or next steps) and provide your preferred contact method. Below is an example of one way to construct a conclusion for your cover letter.

EXAMPLE

Through my education at the University of Kentucky and my experience at the Lexington Theological Seminary, Kentucky State University, the *Georgetown News-Graphic*, and Owen Electric Cooperative, I hope to build stronger information-seeking behaviors across _____ University by not only helping students, staff, and faculty members find the information they need but also by arming them with the skills they need to be good information seekers. I have included my résumé for your review. Please contact me via e-mail at xxxx@xxx.xxx or by phone at 000-000-0000 to schedule an interview to discuss my future contributions to _____ Library and _____ University as systems librarian.

Your signature is optional. Some applicants use a script font for their signature. Some applicants scan their actual signature and use it. Still others omit the signature altogether. Any method is typically acceptable as long as your name closes out the letter.

Additional Application Materials

Some employers may require additional application pieces beyond the cover letter and résumé or CV. This section will review some of those additional pieces.

Required Job Application

Many employers including libraries and library-related organizations require that applicants complete a regular job application. A few of these places may even still require the applicant to complete a paper copy. Most libraries or library-related organizations will have some form of electronic application you can complete and submit for a position. This application typically requires much of the same information that is found on your résumé/CV, but for policy reasons the library or library-related organization is required to obtain and keep a completed application for each applicant. Fortunately for you, some automated application programs will autofill your application if you upload your résumé. The key is to make sure you review each entry on the digital application and make any modifications necessary. More often than not the automated process does not transfer everything properly.

References

Selecting appropriate references is important in the application process. Not all applications will require references, but for those that do it is very important for you to provide references that are knowledgeable about your skills, experience, or education. You can include references on your résumé or CV (not the preferred method), include them as an additional page of your résumé or CV, submit them as part of an employment application, or provide them later upon request.

When identifying potential references, you should consider the following tips:

1. Avoid using family and close friends who are unfamiliar with your professional accomplishments.
2. Select individuals who have supervised you, worked with you on a project or team, or interacted with you in a substantial way.
3. Consider the length of time you have known the person, the amount and types of interactions, and the title of the person when selecting references.
4. Consider the position you are applying for when selecting references. Try to select references who have seen you do work similar or related to the position for which you are applying.
5. Get permission from all references before including them as a reference. If you select a reference who may not be familiar with your recent accomplishments, you may want to provide them with an updated résumé or CV.
6. Stay connected with your references through social media (e.g., LinkedIn) or other means.

7. Consider rotating references if you are actively seeking employment to avoid burnout by references. It is also helpful to have some additional references you can provide in case someone cannot be reached during your search.

Finally, remember that potential employers may look beyond the references you provide. Many times hiring managers may ask their own contacts what they know about applicants. The lesson here is to make sure all of your interactions are professional.

MANAGING APPLICATIONS

The job-hunting and -application process is very intense and information-rich. It can take months to move through the application process, making it challenging for you to remember the details of the jobs and/or specifics of your application materials. This makes it crucial for you to keep copies of your application materials and even job descriptions to ensure better success as you move through the process. This section will focus on ways to keep track of and store your application materials and the job descriptions.

Some applicants question the need to keep their application materials and job descriptions since a digital submission is usually tracked and stored in the employer's application system or in sent e-mails (if the submission is only e-mailed), but this can be ineffective if you are managing and tracking multiple applications.

Keeping Job Descriptions

Sometimes, as stated above, a job description is still available at the application site after submitting the application. Sometimes the job description is removed once the application deadline has passed. This section will take a look at several ways you can track, remember, and access job descriptions after applying.

1. *Store the details mentally.* If you have a photographic memory, then this may be effective. However, it can quickly become challenging

to remember significant details of each position when you are applying for similar positions at multiple libraries.
2. *Print and keep copies of the job description.* If you have access to a printer, this may be a valid option; however, there are a couple of things to keep in mind about printing job descriptions. First, some job boards are not very printer-friendly. A description that should only require two pages may actually print onto three or four pages or cut off content that is outside the printer's margin range. Second, if you are doing a full-blown job search, you may be applying for twenty or more jobs, and that can cost a lot to print.
3. *Store digital copies locally on your computer or in the cloud.* If you can save or print to PDF, this may be a good option for saving job descriptions, as it would give you the opportunity to print the job description later if needed. The biggest drawback with storing digitally would be if your computer died or you lost rights to your cloud account.
4. *Bookmark the job descriptions in your Web browser.* If you have access to the same computer or technological device, then you may be able to save the job description and access it later. The biggest drawback with this method of saving the job description is that you may have limited access to it later if the link becomes unavailable. You also limit the availability of the job description in the event you change computers or need to access the description from another device.
5. *Save the link through Pinterest, del.icio.us, or another social-media or bookmarking site.* If you have certain social-media ac-

---

Pinterest is an online bulletin board where you can digitally pin (save) webpages of interest. You can create boards based on your interests. If you are using Pinterest to store job descriptions, you could create a board call "Job Descriptions" to store all your job descriptions, or you could create multiple boards to group the job descriptions based on specific criteria. You could create a board for jobs based on location. For example, if you are looking for a position at a public library but are open to different locations, you could create a board for different regions or different states.

counts, you may be able to store the job description there. As long as the link is not removed and you remember your password for the associated social-media site, you would continue to have access.

Keeping Application Materials

Since your application materials (cover letter, résumé, or CV) should be customized for each position, it becomes very important to keep multiple copies for later access. You may need to access the materials before an interview, or you may need to share your materials with your references. Either way, keeping the application materials allows you to retrieve them at any time.

There are two primary ways to keep your application materials: digitally or in hard copy. This section will review these options.

1. While not recommended, you could create one generic set of application materials and use it for all applications. This may make it easy to remember what you submitted for each application, but it decreases your chances of success, since your application materials are not customized for each position.
2. You can print all of your application materials for each position and file them alphabetically, based on position or organization. This technique may be effective, but it can get costly if you do not quickly obtain employment.
3. You can store your application materials on each associated job board. This requires you to remember or keep a list of jobs and application sites along with log-in information. This may work if you are only applying to a limited number of libraries or library-related organizations.
4. You can store your application materials on your personal computer or in your cloud account. This can be an effective method for accessing the materials later as long as you do not plan to replace equipment or change cloud accounts. To aid in locating the application materials stored on your computer or in your cloud account, you should start with a consistent naming convention and consider creating folders to group similar application materials together.

> When applying for positions, you should consider including the position title and library name in the file name (e.g., "Reference_NYPL_cover_infotech_NatArchives_resume"). You can include your name as well, but it is not necessarily required anymore, since most job boards rename the document once you upload it.

You should also consider a plan for organizing the files on your computer or in your cloud account. You can put them all in an "Applications" folder and sort them alphabetically or based on the date of application. Or you can create one more level of organization by creating a folder within a folder. You can create a folder for each position and store your résumé and CV, your cover letter, and the job description all in the same folder (see figure 3.1).

However you choose to save your application materials, the key is finding a system that works for you.

Keeping a Log

Whether you keep digital or physical copies of job descriptions and application materials, you should also consider creating a log to inventory all of your application materials. A log can aid in finding your ap-

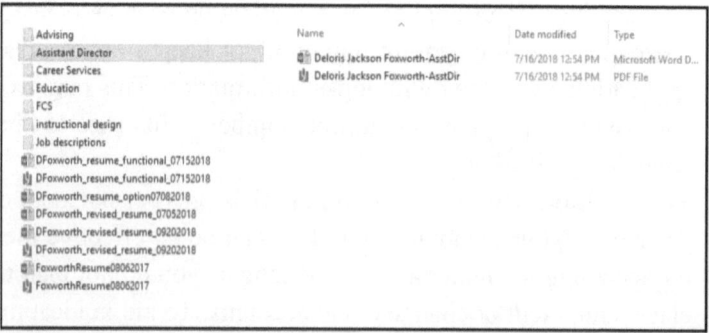

Fig. 3.1. This is a sample of how you can organize your files on your computer to make it easier to find application materials later. Within the folder "Assistant Director" there are two files saved that are related to the application process.
Deloris J. Foxworth

plication materials when you make it to the interview process and want to reread your application materials or the job description. A log may also help keep you from writing each cover letter and résumé or CV from scratch. You can certainly modify existing application materials to submit for other positions if applicable. You can also use ideas or pieces from several different cover letters to create a new letter suitable for a different position. A log may make it easier for you to find related application materials later.

You can create a log on paper or on your computer. The key is to consider what information you want to record early in the process and set up a system that allows for easy additions to the log. It is even better if you create a system that is easily searchable or sortable by position title, date, library or library-related organization, etc.

You should plan to record some key information in the log, including the position title, your application-submission date, the application materials you included (with file names of each document), and the name of the organization to which you applied. You may also consider recording additional information about the closing date of the position (though this is not always available), the contact name (if provided), and any possible questions you have. Finally, you may elect to leave columns or lines to record additional notes, such as interview dates, offers, or other correspondences (application received, processed, referred, etc.).

Table 3.1 shows a log created in Microsoft Excel. The benefit to this log opposed to a handwritten log or a log created as a text-based document is the sorting option that is available. You could sort by any column, filter out certain results, list alphabetically, or list chronologically. If you decide to create a text-based document instead of a spreadsheet, be sure to select a program like Microsoft Word that will allow you to search the document.

NOTES

1. Visit https://www.glassdoor.com/index.htm.
2. Visit https://www.bbb.org.
3. New Mexico State Library, "Library Job Descriptions," accessed December 6, 2018, http://www.nmstatelibrary.org/services-for-nm-libraries/programs-services/librarians-toolkit/library-job-descriptions.

Table 3.1. Applications Log

Position Title	Submission Date	Application Materials	Name of Organization	Closing Date	Contact Name	Questions	Interview Dates	Offer	Feedback
Assistant Director	7/15/2018	Cover letter Résumé Supplemental questions	XYZ Library	7/22/2019			8/12/2019		

4. The Library Corporation, "Sales Engineer," accessed October 14, 2018, https://tlcdelivers.com/job/sales-engineer/ (link no longer active).

5. University of South Carolina, "Event Coordinator," Jobs, accessed September 21, 2018, https://uscjobs.sc.edu/postings/40628 (link no longer active).

6. Ibid.

7. Lincoln County Library System, "Careers at Lincoln County Library," accessed October 14, 2018, https://linclib.org/careers.

8. American Theological Library Association, "Library Director and Media Services," accessed October 14, 2018, cached at https://webcache.googleusercontent.com/search?q=cache:IIB5liwMUBMJ:https://www.atla.com/Members/development/jobs/Pages/Library-Director.aspx+&cd=2&hl=en&ct=clnk&gl=us&client=safari (link no longer active).

9. EBSCO Information Services. "Metadata Librarian I," Careers, accessed October 14, 2018, https://careers.ebscoind.com/ebscoinformation-services/job/Durham-Metadata-Librarian-I-NC-27713/494445300/ (link no longer updated).

10. University of Illinois, "Job Details," Human Resources, accessed October 14, 2018, https://jobs.illinois.edu/faculty-positions/job-details?jobID=103397&job=school-of-information-sciences-senior-lecturer-103397 (link no longer updated).

11. See, respectively, Maine State Library, "Library Job Descriptions," https://www.maine.gov/msl/libs/admin/jobdesc.shtml; New Mexico State Library, "Library Job Descriptions," accessed December 6, 2018, http://www.nmstatelibrary.org/services-for-nm-libraries/programs-services/librarians-toolkit/library-job-descriptions; and Association for Information Science and Technology, "Job Descriptions," accessed December 6, 2018, https://www.asist.org/careers/occupational-paths/job-descriptions/.

12. University of Kentucky, "Equivalencies," Human Resources, accessed December 6, 2018, http://www.uky.edu/hr/employment/working-uk/equivalencies.

13. University of Kentucky, "Data Management Specialist Sr," Jobs, accessed September 16, 2018, https://ukjobs.uky.edu/posting/199582 (page no longer available).

14. Monster, "Should Your Résumé Be in the Past or Present Tense?" Advice, accessed September 21, 2018, https://www.monster.com/career-advice/article/past-or-present-tense.

15. Kim Isaacs, "Is a Combination Résumé Right for You?" Advice, Monster, accessed October 28, 2018, https://www.monster.com/career-advice/article/is-a-combination-resume-right-for-you.

BIBLIOGRAPHY

American Theological Library Association. "Library Director and Media Services." Accessed October 14, 2018. cached at https://webcache.google usercontent.com/search?q=cache:IIB5liwMUBMJ:https://www.atla.com/ Members/development/jobs/Pages/Library-Director.aspx+&cd=2&hl=en& ct=clnk&gl=us&client=safari.

Association for Information Science and Technology. "Job Descriptions." Accessed December 6, 2018. https://www.asist.org/careers/occupational -paths/job-descriptions/.

EBSCO Information Services. "Metadata Librarian I." Careers. Accessed October 14, 2018. https://careers.ebscoind.com/ebscoinformationservices/job/ Durham-Metadata-Librarian-I-NC-27713/494445300/.

Isaacs, Kim. "Is a Combination Résumé Right for You?" Advice. Monster. Accessed October 28, 2019. https://www.monster.com/career-advice/ar ticle/is-a-combination-resume-right-for-you.

The Library Corporation. "Sales Engineer." Accessed October 14, 2018. https://tlcdelivers.com/job/sales-engineer/.

Lincoln County Library System. "Careers at Lincoln County Library." Accessed October 14, 2018. https://linclib.org/careers.

Maine State Library. "Library Job Descriptions." Accessed December 6, 2018. https://www.maine.gov/msl/libs/admin/jobdesc.shtml.

Monster. "Should Your Résumé Be in the Past or Present Tense?" Advice. Accessed September 21, 2018. https://www.monster.com/career-advice/ article/past-or-present-tense.

New Mexico State Library. "Library Job Descriptions." Accessed December 6, 2018. http://www.nmstatelibrary.org/services-for-nm-libraries/programs -services/librarians-toolkit/library-job-descriptions.

University of Illinois. "Job Details." Human Resources. Accessed October 14, 2018. https://jobs.illinois.edu/faculty-positions/job -details?jobID=103397&job=school-of-information-sciences-senior-lec turer-103397.

University of Kentucky. "Data Management Specialist Sr." Jobs. Accessed September 16, 2018. https://ukjobs.uky.edu/posting/199582.

———. "Equivalencies." Human Resources. Accessed December 6, 2018. http://www.uky.edu/hr/employment/working-uk/equivalencies.

University of South Carolina. "Event Coordinator." Jobs. Accessed September 21, 2018. https://uscjobs.sc.edu/postings/40628.

CHAPTER 4

Interviewing for Jobs

Mastering the interview is crucial in the job-searching process. This chapter will help you prepare for the interview. You will learn about some different interview purposes, interview methods, and interview formats. This chapter also has an extensive section on preparing for the interview and ends with a look at the overall interview process.

INTERVIEW PURPOSES

The goal of the interview seems simple. From the employer's perspective, the purpose is to find a suitable candidate. From your perspective, it is to gain reasonable employment. However, upon further investigation the interview purpose is not quite so simple. The interviewers are trying to learn more about you as a candidate, to see what you can contribute to the library or library-related organization, and to possibly even see if you would be a good fit for their culture. Likewise, you are trying to learn more about the library or library-related organization, to convince the interviewers you are the best candidate by sharing your qualifications and interest, and to determine whether the library or library-related organization and the job seem like a good fit for you.

INTERVIEW METHODS

During the application process you are likely to encounter two primary interview methods: technology-assisted and face-to-face. The method can sometimes indicate how far along you are in the hiring process. Some libraries or library-related organizations use technology-assisted interviews for initial screening of candidates with only the top candidates getting a face-to-face interview. Other libraries or library-related organizations may only conduct technology-assisted or face-to-face interviews. However your interview is conducted, know that if you make it to any level of interview you have already impressed the hiring officials.

Technology-Assisted Interviews

Technology-assisted interviews can occur over multiple technological formats. The most common are the telephone or through video chat and conferencing.

Telephone

The telephone interview is the longest-standing technology-assisted interview format. These interviews are often selected because they are relatively cheap to conduct. Phone interviews typically serve as the first in a series of interviews. There are several advantages to this type of interview:

1. You can use and take notes during the interview with minimal disruption or without the interviewer's noticing.
2. You can wear whatever you like.
3. You do not have to make eye contact.
4. You may be able to interview in the comfort of your own home, office, or other familiar space.

There are also some disadvantages to telephone interviews:

1. As with most technology, there is always a chance that the phone will not work.
2. You may not be able to convey certain thoughts or emotions as effectively if you are not able to rely on multiple modes of communication.

3. You do not get to see the campus, branch office, or community where you may be working.

Before your phone interview, review these tips:

- Find a quiet place, free of distractions, for the phone call.
- Arrive to the phone or location for the phone call five to ten minutes early.
- Allow for additional time at the end in case the interview runs over, but do your best to leave the interview on time.
- Avoid using speaker phone if you are the only person on the call.
- Use a landline or VOIP phone to minimize the chance of losing the call.
- If using a cellular phone, make sure it is sufficiently charged.
- Try to respond as though you are participating in a face-to-face interview, but understand you are limited to only your voice in conveying messages.
- If you have to call in for the interview, plan to call a few minutes (no more than five to ten minutes) before the scheduled interview time. This is important in case you have any difficulties when trying to call.

Computer-Mediated Interviews

Video chat and conferencing is becoming the technology of choice by hiring officials because it most closely simulates the face-to-face interview but is usually cheaper to conduct. Some libraries or library-related organizations will use this method to conduct initial screenings, while others will use this to conduct final interviews. Most libraries or library-related organizations make the decision based on multiple considerations. Some of the top considerations are location of the interviewee in relation to the interviewers, the interviewers' location in relation to each other, the funding to host interviewees on site, or to test the technology know-how of the applicant.

Interviews conducted by video chat or conferencing are typically held live with the interviewer(s) and interviewee over the Internet. You should plan to use a computer with a microphone, webcam, and speakers during the interview. Below are some tips you should consider when participating in a computer-mediated interview:

- Be sure to locate adequate technology hardware for the interview. Test all computers, microphones, speakers, etc., to make sure they are working appropriately.
- Download any needed software or apps to your computer. Test the software or app to make sure it works correctly with your hardware.
- Minimize distractions in your interview space and/or plan your interview in a private space.
- Plan to have your technology set up five to ten minutes before the scheduled interview. This includes logging in to any designated software (e.g., Skype, GoToMeeting, Zoom, Google Hangouts).
- Plan extra time before and after the interview in case the interview runs over or you experience any technical difficulties.
- If you are using a laptop, tablet, or smartphone, make sure it is sufficiently charged.
- You are expected to make eye contact or give the illusion of eye contact in a computer-mediated video interview. To achieve this illusion, look at the webcam attached to your computer, phone, or tablet instead of the eyes of the interviewers on-screen.

While most computer-mediated interviews are conducted in real time, one of the latest technology-assisted interviews, the "selfie" or "one-way" interview, is a prerecorded interview you submit to the library or library-related organization. In this type of interview you visually record your response to a predetermined set of questions. A library or library-related organization may require this type of interview to test your technology skills, communication skills, reactions, response time, stress management, etc. They may also utilize this type of interview to expand the applicant pool without incurring more cost to host interviews.

However your computer-mediated interview is conducted, there are a number of advantages to the computer-mediated interview:

1. You can demonstrate your technology skills.
2. You may be able to pick up on certain visual cues during the interview that you may not have noticed in a telephone interview.

3. You may be able to interview in the comfort of your own home, office, or other familiar space.

There are also some disadvantages to computer-mediated interviews:

1. When you participate in an interview conducted via video chat or conferencing, you must maintain almost the same standards as you would in a face-to-face interview.
2. You must have the technical skills and access to appropriate equipment for the interview.
3. You have to continuously remember to look at the webcam on your computer instead of the eyes of the interviewer(s) on the screen.
4. You must make certain you are dressed appropriately for an interview.
5. You do not get to see the campus, branch office, or community where you may be working.

Face-to-Face Interviews

Face-to-face interviews are typically held before final hiring decisions are made and may be in addition to or in place of technology-assisted interviews. These interviews can happen one-on-one (with interviewer and interviewee), as a panel or group, or over multiple smaller interviews with a variety of people connected to the library or library-related organization.

There are several advantages to face-to-face meetings over the other meeting formats:

1. You are less likely to have to demonstrate technology skills or use technology during the interview.
2. You may receive a tour of the library or facility where you will be working and may get to see your workspace.
3. You may get to meet and interact with possible supervisors or coworkers.

Similarly there are several disadvantages to face-to-face meetings:

1. You may be judged (consciously or unconsciously) on your appearance.

2. You may be judged (consciously or unconsciously) on your handshake.
3. You will be expected to make eye contact with all interviewers.
4. You may not be able to take or review notes during the interview.

Before your face-to-face interview, review these tips:

1. Make sure you are presentable. Proper attire is addressed toward the end of this chapter.
2. Plan to bring extra copies of your application materials to share with the hiring officials (upon request, of course).
3. Turn your phone off—or at least turn the volume off—and put your phone out of sight.
4. Plan to arrive five to ten minutes before your scheduled interview time.
5. Be respectful of all office staff. Many times hiring personnel seek the opinions of receptionists and other staff who may casually interact with the candidates.
6. Make eye contact with all interviewers.
7. Be sure to make a mental note of interviewer(s) names and to refer to the interviewer(s) by name at least one time.

INTERVIEW FORMAT

No matter the type of interview you land, you should ask about the interview format to be better prepared. This section will review some of the most common interview formats.

One-on-One Interviews

One-on-one interviews may be conducted by the primary decision maker in the hiring process. In a library this may be the library director, branch manager, department manager, or human resources professional. Outside a library this may be a supervisor, manager, or human resources representative. Keep in mind that in many cases the person conducting a one-on-one interview may not be the final decision maker but, rather, someone who informs on the hiring decision. The key is for you to treat the interviewer, no matter their credentials, as though the decision were solely theirs.

Below are some tips to help you succeed in a one-on-one interview:

1. Make eye contact with the interviewer, but look away occasionally to make it seem more normal.
2. Call the interviewer by name when appropriate.
3. Pace yourself, and even consider restating the question in your own words to help you better organize your response.

Panel Interviews

Panel interviews consist of multiple interviewers and one interviewee. An interview with multiple interviewers may be intimidating, but it does not have to be. Below are some tips to help you succeed when being interviewed by a group:

1. Treat all interviewers equally, no matter their rank. All interviewers will likely have a say in the final hiring decision.
2. When responding to a question, be sure to focus on the interviewer who posed the question, but do not forget to look around at the other interviewers through the course of the answer.
3. Take note of the names of all the interviewers, and refer to the interviewers by name when possible.

Group Interviews

Group interviews are less common because they require multiple candidates to interview at the same time. This type of interview is conducted not to pit you against your competition but, rather, to see how you interact with others. In this type of interview it is important that you try not to outshine the other candidates. Instead, you should be listening to their responses, acknowledging good ideas when appropriate, and building on others' responses instead of repeating their responses. Group interviews are quite different, so these tips may help you succeed in this type of group interview:

1. Treat the other interviewees with the same respect as the interviewer(s).
2. Be sure to make eye contact with the interviewer(s).

3. Take note of the names of the interviewer(s) and the other interviewees, and refer to them when appropriate.
4. Try not to dominate the interview. Make sure all interviewees get ample opportunity to respond.
5. Always try to incorporate and/or add to the other interviewees' responses when appropriate.
6. Avoid saying your ideas are better than another interviewee's.

Presentation Interviews

In presentation interviews, you are asked to deliver a prepared presentation. This is usually in addition to one of the other interview formats and may be used to test your knowledge on a topic, your presentation skills, and your preparation skills. Your presentation may occur only in front of the interviewers, or it may occur in front of an audience of other library employees, library patrons, or other audiences.

If you are interviewing for an academic-library job, you may be asked to deliver an information-literacy presentation you would present to students. If you are interviewing to be a children's librarian, you may be asked to read a story or deliver a whole story-time program. If you are interviewing to be a sales representative for a library vendor, you may be asked to deliver a sales pitch to a potential library client.

The key to a successful presentation interview is preparation, if possible. If you know you are going to have to give a presentation, be sure to research, plan, and rehearse your presentation before arriving for your interview. If you are put on the spot, try to make eye contact and pace yourself. Remember, it does not have to be perfect: making a mistake actually allows you to show how you can recover in times of stress. Just do your best.

Combination Interviews

Many times any one of these interview formats is not exclusive, meaning you may go to one interview and participate in multiple interview formats. As previously stated, this is likely to occur with a presentation interview. Not only will you be asked to present, but you will also likely participate in a one-on-one or panel interview.

Academic-library interviews are a common example of the combined format for an interview. Academic-library interviews are typically day-long interviews (including additional days for travel to and from the interview site) requiring you to meet with a variety of people at different levels within the college or university and the library. You may interact with human resource screeners, administrative staff, library and college or university faculty, students, library and college or university administrators, and more. You will also be expected to interact with the interviewers in a variety of different contexts. You will likely participate in one-on-one interviews, panel interviews, a presentation interview, and less-formal interview settings such as travel to and around campus and meals. Academic libraries use this holistic interview process to learn more about your skills, knowledge, and experience while also observing how you interact with others and perform in a variety of stressful situations. The College of Law Library at the University of Illinois offers a typical interview schedule for an academic-library position:

- Day 1: Arrive at airport. Dinner with representatives from department.
- Day 2: Early morning pickup at hotel.
  - Associate director meeting (30 minutes)
  - Dean meeting (25 minutes)
  - HR representatives (30 minutes
  - Presentation preparation (30 minutes)
  - Presentation to faculty, staff, and students invited (1.5 hours)
  - Meeting with librarians (50 minutes)
  - Meeting with campus promotion and tenure representatives (30 minutes)
  - Meeting with university librarian (30 minutes)
  - Meeting with library director (1 hour)
- Day 3: Tour of city with staff representative (1 hour)[1]

PREPARING FOR YOUR INTERVIEW

Landing an interview is an important step in the job-application process, but there is much work still to be done in order to get the job. You will need to spend adequate time preparing for the interview.

You should start preparing as soon as you accept the interview. There are certain key pieces of information you should confirm.

1. Confirm the location and format of the interview.
    a. If the interview is in person, don't just assume it will be at the main library or headquarters. It could be at the main location, a branch location, a professional conference, or even some other designated location. It is very important to ask.
    b. Is the interview going to be technology-assisted? If so, will you use the phone, computer, etc.? If over the phone, will the interviewer call you, or should you call them? If online using Skype or other video-conferencing or -calling software, do you have an account or access to the software? Will you need to update your computer equipment by adding software or additional hardware (e.g., microphone or headphones)? If so, it is important to make any technology updates ahead of time and test the software and hardware to be used prior to the interview.
2. Confirm who will be conducting the interview. Will it be one person or multiple people? Try to learn as much as you can about each of the interviewers before the interview.
3. Confirm their expectations about the interview. How long will the interview last? What is the purpose of this interview? Will you be interviewing with other interviewees? Do you have to do a presentation?

In the days leading up to the interview, you should research, plan, and practice for the interview.

Research for the Interview

You should research the library or library-related organization and any affiliated organizations or associations, review the job description and your application materials, investigate similar positions at other libraries or library-related organizations, and familiarize yourself with key concepts and major issues related to the type of library or library-related organization where interviewing.

1. You should visit the library or library-related organization's website. You should read the mission statement and purpose; learn as much as you can about applicable programs, products, and

services; review the staff, board of directors, and community and corporate partners (vendors); etc.
2. You should try to identify affiliated organizations and associations and understand their relationship with the library or library-related organization. Affiliated organizations and associations may include state library associations, consortiums, cooperatives, and even library vendors. The Online Computer Library Center, Inc., (OCLC) is an example of a cooperative of libraries that participate in resource sharing through WorldCat. If you are interviewing for an interlibrary-loan position, it may be important to know what both OCLC and WorldCat are and how they help libraries.
3. You should review your application materials and the job description. You need to make sure you are knowledgeable both about the job description and your qualifications as they relate to the position. In the job description you should pay particular attention to the skills and experience required and to the specific duties of the job. In your application materials you should pay particular attention to specific examples you included in your cover letter, as an interviewer may refer to your letter. You should also look over your résumé to make sure you are knowledgeable of all your previous experience and skills. An interviewer could potentially ask a question related to any one of your previous positions.
4. You should also research the career field. You can search for and read about similar types of positions in other libraries or library-related organizations by visiting professional associations, competitor websites, or publications like the Bureau of Labor Statistics *Occupational Outlook Handbook*.[2] You should be familiar with the duties, average salary, working conditions, required education, and hiring outlook for similar positions. This information may prove valuable during your interview.
5. You should familiarize yourself with key library or library-related concepts that are related to the position. For example, if you are interviewing to be a metadata librarian, you want to make sure you are familiar with the current encoding schemes (e.g., MARC 21) or content-encoding schemes (e.g., AACR2, RDA) relevant

for the hiring library. You should also familiarize yourself with big issues related to the position and library or library-related organization. For example, if you are interviewing to be a collection-development librarian, it may be important to be familiar with the current state of digital-rights management and its impact on e-book distribution to libraries. Being knowledgeable about concepts and issues pertinent to the hiring organization can help you answer interview questions designed to test your knowledge in the field.

Plan for the Interview

After researching, the next step is planning. You should plan for the interview by reviewing potential questions, planning possible answers, and generating your own questions to ask during the interview.

Review Interview Questions

You can find an abundance of sample interview questions on the Internet. Below is a brief explanation of some library-specific resources that share interview questions you may encounter in a library or library-related job interview:

- Hiring Librarians provides job seekers a wealth of information to aid in the job search. One key resource is their interview-question repository.[3] When you access this resource you will find actual questions other job seekers have encountered in interviews.
- San José State University's School of Information provides sample behavioral-interview questions and provides a brief description of the STAR method—Situation, Task, Action, Result—with example responses.[4]
- The Florida State University Libraries created a research guide specifically for library and technology jobs and associated interview questions. This research guide (guides.lib.fsu.edu/c.php?g=352933&p=2383379) provides links to a number of online resources for sample questions, information about illegal or inappropriate questions, asking questions as the interviewee, sample questions, and recommendations for answer preparation.[5]

- The blog *INALJ* (formerly *I Need a Library Job*) provides multiple articles related to interview questions, including describing behavioral interviewing, reviewing what types of questions to expect, reviewing the STAR method, and providing some sample "tricky" questions you may encounter in your interview.[6]
- The Public Library Association provides examples of general and library-specific interview questions.[7]
- The *Mr. Library Dude* blog shares a list of resources that offer interview questions, ranging from educational institutions like the University of North Carolina at Chapel Hill and the University of Washington to library associations like the Illinois Library Association, among many other resources.[8]
- Drexel University groups sample interview questions by topic: questions about you, about your skills and motivation, about your experience, and about hypothetical situations and theoretical questions. You can also find sample questions you can consider asking in the interview.[9]
- Indiana Library Federation provides a collection of resources that offer sample interview questions.[10]
- The University of Washington's (UW) Information School provides frequently asked interview questions, along with tips on how to respond. UW also provides a list of sample interview questions and identifies the types of libraries and jobs that might use each question.[11]
- The American Library Association provides a summary of the academic interview process and includes a number of potential interview questions.[12]
- The University of North Carolina's University Library provides some sample interview questions organized by skill or purpose of the question.[13]

Most interview questions, no matter the source, can be categorized as behavioral, situational, or general and are used to gather information about your knowledge, skills, or abilities.[14] Behavioral questions are used to attempt to predict future behavior by asking you to elaborate on your past behavior. Behavioral questions allow you to confirm you have experience in the area in question and that you can apply past experience to a new situation. Situational questions are hypothetical and

> General interview questions can vary tremendously. Here is one general interview question that sometimes catches interviewees off guard:
>
> QUESTION: What books are you currently reading or have you read recently? Would you recommend one or more of those books, and, if so, why?
>
> Answer Tips: To answer this question effectively, you should be prepared to share title and author information and a general summary of one or more books that you have recently read. Your goal should be to get the interviewers interested in the book(s) and demonstrate knowledge and skills you have about reader's advisory. Ultimately the interviewers are less interested in what you are reading and more interested in your description and recommendation of the book(s).

used to find out how you would react to a certain situation. You should answer these questions by elaborating on how you would react if faced with a certain scenario. Responses to situational questions do not have to be based on actual experience but can be if you believe the experience is relevant to the question being asked. General questions encompass all other types of questions and may include direct questions about your knowledge, skills, or abilities or may also include questions about your interests and goals.

Due to the sheer number of potential interview questions, preparing for an interview can be an agonizing experience. However, there are ways to make your preparation more productive. Instead of simply going through the list of questions on one (or multiple) website(s), you should try to focus on your own skills, knowledge, and experience and how those relate to the job and the library or library-related organization. The next section will introduce you to a planning process and tools you can use to better prepare yourself for your interview.

Plan Responses

Before delving into possible interview questions, you should compile two lists. First, you should make a list of your own skills, knowledge (key library- and information-related terminology), and experiences. Remember, you may have highlighted some of these on your application materials, but you need to think beyond what you have already shared in your application materials. What other skills do you have? These can be more general skills like interpersonal communication, teamwork, and computer skills, in addition to very position-specific skills like knowing how to use a bibliographic-reference manager. Next, you should make a list of key skills and terminology identified in the actual job description and similar job descriptions. You should include in this list any skills or terminology (e.g., technology resources) you identified when you reviewed the library or library-related organization's website.

Then compare your skills/knowledge/experience list with those elements you identified from job descriptions and the website. How do the two lists compare? Hopefully you see some common elements. If so, you should try to focus on those aspects as you move forward in planning responses. If not, then you may need to further evaluate your skills and experience to find similarities to the job descriptions. Remember, you made it to the interview, so the connections exist, you may just need to think more about your experience and education to find them.

Finally, combine the two lists, keeping the duplicated skills and concepts at the top of the new list. Once completed, set the list aside. You will use this new list to start planning possible responses. However, before you can plan responses, you need a method to follow. One of the most popular response planning methods is the STAR method (similar methods are the CAR, PAR, and SARA methods, among others).

The STAR method helps you plan responses to behavioral and situational interview questions so that you can make sure your responses are concise and focused. In the STAR method you share examples from your previous experience or education to demonstrate your skills and knowledge related to a specific concept or situation. To share successfully, you need to include each element of the STAR acronym, presented below:

- *Situation.* You should provide a brief description of the condition, problem, or situation that warrants action.
- *Task.* You should provide a brief description of the identified task to address the condition, problem, or situation.
- *Action.* You should identify the specific actions or role you played in addressing the condition, problem, or situation.

- *Result.* You should summarize the outcomes of the tasks and actions. This can be personal or organizational accomplishments or lessons learned.

Combing the STAR method with your earlier list, you should now construct a fillable spreadsheet or grid (see table 4.1). First, enter your earlier list of skills and knowledge in a column on the far left of a Microsoft Excel or Google Sheets spreadsheet—or on a piece of lined paper if you prefer to do this by hand. Second, add the four STAR elements in a row across the top of the spreadsheet. This layout is similar to the skills matrix used by career centers at Texas A&M and the University of Kentucky.

This is a useful tool as you start planning out responses to possible interview questions. In some ways it is more helpful than simply reading questions and constructing responses. By building this spreadsheet you are able to consider skills and knowledge outside of the question context. This may help you develop examples from your past that you may miss by focusing on a specific question. It can also help you develop more examples from your past if you make yourself develop a different situation, task, or action related to each skill or concept you've identified on your list or if you make multiple examples for each identified skill. Without question, by developing at least one STAR response for each identified skill or library-related concept (Texas A&M and the University of Kentucky suggest developing multiple examples) you will be better prepared for your interview.

When answering any type of interview questions, there are certain things you should avoid:

1. Avoid identifying coworkers, supervisors, customers, users, or patrons by name. This is important, because it demonstrates your values related to privacy and confidentiality. Whether it is maintaining circulation records for a patron at a public library or using customer data to personalize a shopper's experience, data privacy is a top priority for many libraries or library-related organizations.
2. Avoid talking negatively about the library or library-related organization, its employees, vendors, or clients. This may be challenging,

Table 4.1. STAR Planning Tool

Skill	Situation	Task	Action	Result
Collection development	The library contacted the Department of Fine Arts seeking recommended titles to expand its collection related to communication titles.	I was tasked with submitting a list of new communication-related titles for purchase.	I conducted a quick review of the library's communication offerings. I searched communication professional-development-association resources and book reviews for new/upcoming titles and compiled a list of titles with cost and publisher information.	The library added $1,000-worth of new titles from my list.
Strategic planning	The library was planning to submit an e-rate funding request that required that a technology-management plan be on file with the state library association.	Since the library did not have a technology plan, I was tasked with developing a five-year technology plan.	I worked in conjunction with the library director to develop a list of technology needs/priorities for the library. After reviewing multiple technology plans online, I wrote a plan for the library.	The technology plan was recognized as one of the best in the state and was sufficient for the library to secure e-rate funding through the federal government.

(continued)

Table 4.1. (Continued)

Skill	Situation	Task	Action	Result
Supervising	One of the library's leadership teams needed to take an extended leave from the library.	The library needed someone to cover the librarian's supervisory shifts during their leave.	I supervised between five and seven library workers one night a week and every third weekend for over two months. I was responsible for opening and closing procedures, assigning shift responsibilities, and addressing any complaints by patrons or employees.	Because I filled in as supervisor during the extended leave, the library was able to operate with minimal disruptions to staff schedules and responsibilities.
Teamwork				
Editing bibliographic data				
Planning				
Presenting				
Problem solving				

Note: This is similar to the skills matrices used by career centers at Texas A&M University and the University of Kentucky.
Source: University of Kentucky, Lewis Honors College, "Skills Matrix," accessed November 28, 2018, http://www.uky.edu/honors/sites/www.uky.edu.honors/files/Skills%20Matrix.pdf.

Here are some sample interview questions with sample responses and notes you can review to help you better prepare for your interview. While these questions may or may not be included in your interview, reviewing them and the associated notes can help you become more comfortable applying the information in your STAR planning tool.

The first two examples are compound questions that easily fit the STAR method.

QUESTION 1: Describe a project you worked on that involved collaborating with community leaders or outside organizations. What went well? What didn't? What did you learn about partnering with other organizations?[15]

NOTE: Using the STAR method, you should focus on your role in a collaborative project you have worked on in a previous position. If you have not held a professional position, then think about work you did on volunteer or group projects that demonstrates collaboration, even if not with community leaders or organizations. Whatever example you provide, be sure to briefly describe the situation and task before identifying your role (specific actions) and the outcomes (results) of the collaborative efforts. Be sure to avoid criticizing community leaders, outside organizations, or internal collaborators. Instead, concentrate on your own behaviors and lessons learned during the process. Below is one example response.

RESPONSE 1: While teaching an introductory course in information communication technology (ICT), I wanted to share real-world examples with students through a speaker series. To make this happen, I had to identify and contact potential speakers and invite them to speak in person or virtually. Then I had to coordinate their visits or presentations with the departmental administrative assistant, technology consultant, and marketing assistant to schedule, record, and promote the series. Over two semesters, the speaker series saw some successes and some challenges. During the first semester, the series was very successful, with ten speakers. The second semester, there were some slight challenges, as some speakers were not available the second time around. However, since the technology consultant had helped me record each speaker the first semester, I was able to share the videos when I was not able to secure a speaker for a certain topic. The second semester I hosted eight speakers and used two previously recorded videos. Through the two speaker series I learned how important it is to plan early, identify backup speakers, and record all special presentations.

QUESTION 2: What's an example of a time you used your fact-finding skills to gain information needed to solve a problem? How did you analyze the information and come to a decision?[16]

NOTE: Your answer to this question will likely be used to evaluate your research abilities and your customer-service skills. It may be tempting to start listing searching techniques and tools you learned about through your education or experience. However, you'll notice the question is asking for a specific example. Instead of trying to show your vast knowledge of tools or techniques, try to identify and share one specific example that highlights your knowledge and skills in information finding while helping solve a problem. Start by outlining the situation and task. Then identify the specific task(s) you performed. Finally, share the results from your efforts.

RESPONSE 2: I once observed a parent attempting to help their child find sources for a homework assignment. The student and parent were using a computer to find information on the Internet. Realizing the parent and student seemed unsure of where to look, I conducted a brief reference interview to learn more about the assignment and the specific information needs of the student. After learning the student was working on a class assignment, I showed the student how to use the library's electronic databases and demonstrated Gale Virtual Reference Library and ProQuest.

The next example is still a behavioral question, but the question is different from the first questions in that it does not directly suggest components of the STAR method. Regardless, you should still plan to use the STAR method as a guide when answering these types of questions.

QUESTION 3: What's something innovative you've done in your current job (or coursework, etc.)?[17]

NOTE: While you could simply share an example of something innovative you've done, your response would be more memorable and effective if you describe the situation that led to the need for the innovation and then identified the task and your role in implementing the innovation (action). Additionally, if you can share the results or lessons learned from the implementation of the innovation (results), you will certainly make an impression on the interviewers. Below is a sample response using the STAR method. This is a much stronger response than simply saying "I started a device club to help patrons learn more about their iPads."

RESPONSE 3: In response to the growing number of patron questions about iPad features, I started a device club that worked similarly to a book club. In an attempt to establish a core group of attendees, I personally invited patrons who had attended a previous iPad workshop or whom I knew had an iPad. The first event was well attended. The attendees even asked to meet more than once a month.

Remember, these are just examples. Try to refer back to your STAR planning tool when answering behavioral questions. You want to demonstrate relevant skills and knowledge through vivid examples.

especially when you have a negative impression of or experience with a coworker or supervisor, but remember that placing blame or talking negatively about another may actually suggest an inability to get along with others.
3. Avoid being unreasonably positive. It is acceptable and often encouraged to share a failure you experienced on the job. It is important to make sure you indicate to the interviewer how you resolved the issue and what you learned through the experience.
4. Avoid sharing personal stories or examples. Try to keep all examples professional, educational, or service-oriented. There are some exceptions to this, however.
    a. One special case might be if you have been a stay-at-home parent for several years and the interview question deals with skills such as managing schedules, assigning tasks, prioritizing, etc. Parents typically have extensive experience in these areas even when they do not realize it.
    b. Another exception might be if your volunteer experience does not tie directly to library or information science and rather is very personal. For example, if you have been coordinating food service for your son or daughter's marching band for the last two years, the organizational and interpersonal skills you are using may be very transferrable to the library or library-related position you are seeking.

Plan Questions

It is always important to have some of your own questions planned for the interview. In most interviews a few minutes at the end will be reserved for you, the interviewee, to ask questions. This is significant and is considered part of your interview. You should plan to ask questions that further demonstrate your knowledge, preparation, and interest while also addressing position-related concerns you have. You should avoid asking questions about salary, working hours, vacation or other benefits, or workplace rumors. Many of these types of questions can be addressed in final negotiations before accepting a job.

You should plan at least one question on current events or industry topics relevant to the library or library-related organization. These questions can demonstrate your knowledge of current events and issues related to the library, library-related organization, and industry.

Below are sample questions regarding current events or industry topics. You will want to confirm these are applicable to the position, library, or library-related organization before asking any of them in an interview setting:

1. Many schools like Kansas State University and the University of Kentucky offer grants or resources to help faculty find and adopt free (or reduced-cost) alternative textbooks. Does this library have a statement or position related to alternative textbooks?
2. There is a growing trend to scan and store IDs, library cards, and customer loyalty cards on a smartphone. What is the library's position on this use of technology by its users? Will the library accept digital copies of a library card?
3. There has been a lot in the news about the circulation of 3-D gun blueprints available online. Does the library have policies or procedures in place to restrict what can be printed in the library's new makerspace?

You should plan to ask at least one question about recent or current projects conducted by the department, the library or library-related organization, or a similar organization. These questions can demonstrate that you have conducted research specific to the hiring library or library-related organization.

Below are sample questions based on current or recent projects by particular libraries. You will want to confirm your interviewing library or library-related organization is working on or has completed these projects before asking these questions in an interview setting:

1. As a member of the community I know that the library currently operates two Library Express (locker and kiosk systems) sites in smaller communities out in the county. What are the library's plans to expand these services, and what role would this position have in this expansion?
2. I noticed that the library has an online information-literacy course students can enroll in and complete on their own. How have the students (and faculty) responded to this course?

3. The library currently offers access to three electronic databases for students. Are there plans to partner with the public library or another resource to expand the electronic offerings to students?

You can plan to ask at least one question about specific job duties. These questions can demonstrate your knowledge of the position.

Below are sample questions related to specific job descriptions. You will want to confirm that they appropriately relate to an aspect of the job for which you are interviewing or are mentioned in the job description before asking these questions in an interview setting:

1. One of the duties outlined in the job description was coordinating volunteers. Does the library require volunteers to have background checks? If so, would I be responsible for getting those done?
2. The job description indicates that my time would be split among two different branches. Do you have a current breakdown of how my time would be divided among branches?
3. As a library faculty member, what research or publication requirements and service requirements would I need to meet annually and for promotion and tenure?

You can plan to ask at least one question regarding the hiring process. One to two questions related to the hiring process can demonstrate that you are still interested in the position following the interview segment.

Below are sample questions regarding the hiring process. You will want to make sure the questions are applicable and have not already been addressed before asking any of these questions in an interview setting:

1. You have indicated that you hope to have a decision by the end of next week. How do you plan to follow up with me?
2. If I have additional questions, whom should I contact? Can I send those questions directly to you (identifying the search chair by name), or should I submit those questions to the search coordinator (identifying this person by name, if known)?
3. When do you expect to have someone in this position?

There are a number of other acceptable questions you can ask that do not necessarily demonstrate your knowledge, skills, or interest related to the position. While it is okay to ask these questions if necessary, you should limit these questions.

The questions below are not all-inclusive and may not be appropriate in all interviews. Please use these as you see fit.

1. Is there funding for professional development? You can tailor this question even more by indicating a particular professional association and/or conference. For example, if you are interviewing for a youth-services public-library position, you might rephrase the question to something like the following. YALSA is the premiere organization for youth services. Would the library provide funding to attend the annual conference?
2. What do you find most rewarding about working for (insert the name of the library or library-related organization)?
3. Is there much collaboration in the office? Can you provide a specific example?

You also need to keep in mind that there are some questions that are not acceptable for this stage of the interview. For example, while salary or other benefits may be a huge concern, you should not ask about them at this time. Wait until you are offered the job before trying to negotiate or ask about these things. You should avoid asking the interviewer(s) personal questions about their family or religious beliefs since this is a professional interview. You should also avoid asking about relationships among employees and/or supervisors or challenges they face in their work since this may likely put the interviewer(s) on the spot.

Practice for the Interview

You may feel silly, but after reviewing your completed skills matrix and your questions to ask, you should practice. Practice with talking points, not a written script.[18] The goal is to sound conversational, not rehearsed. By practicing talking points, you should feel more comfortable with your responses when delivering and/or altering them during the actual interview. Practicing talking points and your matrix instead of responses to specific questions should also help you feel more confident even when asked a question you did not rehearse.

There are a number of ways you can practice to feel more comfortable during the interview:

1. You can share some questions from the resources identified earlier in this chapter with a friend and ask them to ask you each question so you can practice responding.
2. You can identify some possible questions and video your responses to each question. Then you can evaluate your own responses. Think about what you were most comfortable with. What seemed to come naturally? What seemed artificial? Could you detect the use of each element of the STAR method in your response? If not, how can you improve your response?
3. You can practice in a mirror. Remember, eye contact is very important in a face-to-face interview. A mirror can be a good way to practice if you do not have a friend available to help.

FINAL PREPARATIONS

You should use the night before and the morning of the interview to prepare mentally and physically for the interview. This includes getting adequate rest, selecting appropriate attire, grooming properly, and eating adequately.

- *Adequate rest.* You should plan to maintain your regular sleep schedule the night before your interview. You don't want to get significantly more or less sleep than you normally get, as this may make you feel extremely groggy or irritable during your interview.
- *Proper attire.* You should plan to dress appropriately for the job interview. "Appropriate" is traditionally defined as one level of dress above the regularly accepted dress code for the job. This means that if the regular dress for the library or library-related organization is business casual, then you should dress business professional for the job interview. When in doubt, err on the side of being overdressed rather than underdressed. A good, quality suit or nice dress clothes indicate you are serious about the position.

- *Grooming.* You should plan to be groomed appropriately. If you are unsure what is appropriate, err on the conservative side or visit the library or library-related organization ahead of time to determine what appears to be acceptable.
- *Eat adequately.* You should plan to maintain your regular eating schedule the day of an interview. Don't go overboard and try to eat a large breakfast if you normally skip breakfast. Similarly, if you normally eat breakfast, don't skip it. As you may be nervous during your interview, you don't want to present another reason to be nervous or uncomfortable.

DURING THE INTERVIEW

You are as prepared as you can be. It's now time for the interview. What should you expect? Typically there is a predictable format most interviews follow (academic interviews are slightly different and discussed separately). There will be a brief introduction period, a question-and-answer session during which you will be expected to answer questions, an opportunity for you to ask questions, and a "next steps" segment from the interviewer(s).

The introduction will usually consist of handshakes (if in person) and brief introductions of the interviewer(s). Typically, they will share their name, title, and connection to the position or hiring committee. You should try to make eye contact and repeat the person's name as they introduce themselves. Following their introductions, the interviewer(s) will likely ask you to tell a little about yourself at this time. If so, you should briefly tell who you are, your title, if you have one (or brief qualification for the job), and why you are interested in the position. Avoid sharing personal information about your family, personal life, political or religious beliefs, and the like. If the interviewer(s) does not ask for an introduction, you may elect to make a brief introduction statement and wait for further instruction or questions.

Once the introductions have concluded, the questions usually commence. This is your moment to shine. You will likely find yourself doing a lot of the talking, and that is acceptable as long as it is focused. Make sure you listen to the questions and think about your preparation work before answering. Some interviewees try to buy themselves a little more time by repeating the question. Instead of repeating the question, try to rephrase the question as a statement to start your response. This is more constructive, as it shows you understand the question and it allows you another split second to think on your response.

During the question segment, keep in mind that most interviews use a standard list of questions that were agreed upon before the interviews started. The interviewer's goal is to get through all of those questions. Knowing this, it is crucial that you keep your answers brief and focused. This is where the STAR method and your preplanning will benefit you. Refer back to earlier in this chapter to refresh yourself on using the STAR method.

You also need to keep in mind that there are some questions that interviewers are not allowed to ask. You should not be asked direct questions about your marital and parental status, religious affiliations, gender identity, sexual preference, or personal opinion on a particular population or behavior. If you are asked questions on these topics, you should politely refrain from answering them. You can respond in a number of ways:

1. You can simply say you do not feel comfortable answering that question.
2. You can ask how the question is relevant to the position.
3. You can simply try to turn the focus of the question back to the library or library-related organization or position. For example, if you are asked where you go to church, you can respond by acknowledging significance of churches as community partners. For example, the Scott County Public Library in Georgetown, Kentucky, has partnered with local church daycares to reach more preschool students through on-site story times. Other libraries might choose to partner with churches as a bookmobile stop, a host for community workshops, etc.

Most interviews will allow some time at the end for you to ask questions. This is where the plan-questions section of this chapter comes in handy. You should definitely be prepared to ask some questions, but know that you may or may not get the opportunity to ask all of the questions. With this in mind, try to mix the questions based on what you must know with what demonstrates your knowledge and interest in the position.

Before the interview officially ends, sometimes an interviewer will provide a brief comment about the interview process. This is sometimes labeled "next steps," as they often provide a timeline as to when they will make the decision and contact you following the interview. If they do not provide this information, you may ask this question.

When you are leaving the interview, you should politely thank all interviewers for their time. If you are in a face-to-face interview, you should extend your hand to each interviewer and thank them personally. If you can remember each interviewers' name, include their name. If not, thank them for their time, shake their hand, and, if it seems appropriate, ask again for their name. If the interview is computer-mediated, then briefly thank them for their time. In all instances you might try to leave them with a memorable statement or last thought. Just make sure that it is not too over-the-top and, more importantly, that it represents you and reiterates why you should be their top candidate or strongly indicates your desire to make it to the next step.

NOTES

1. Adapted from University of Illinois, College of Law Library, "LIS 530 GLE: Legal Resources: The Interview Process," last updated December 4, 2018, https://libguides.law.illinois.edu/c.php?g=494760&p=3685748.

2. The Bureau of Labor Statistics, "Occupational Outlook Handbook," last modified April 13, 2018, https://www.bls.gov/ooh/.

3. For example, see Emily Weak, search results for "Interview Questions Repository," *Hiring Librarians* (blog), accessed December 6, 2018, https://hiringlibrarians.com/?s=Interview+Questions+Repository.

4. San José State University, School of Information, "Behavioral Interview Questions." Accessed September 25, 2018, https://ischool.sjsu.edu/behavioral-interview-questions.

5. Florida State University Libraries, "Library and Technology Jobs: Library Interview Questions," last updated May 5, 2017, http://guides.lib.fsu.edu/c.php?g=352933&p=2383379.

6. Brad McNally, "Behavioral Interviews (And How You Can Use Them to Your Advantage)," *INALJ*, April 7, 2014, http://inalj.com/?p=67484; and Ruth Lincoln, "Conflict in the Job Interview: How to Approach the Tricky Questions," *INALJ*, October 4, 2013, and August 29, 2014, http://inalj.com/?p=42145.

7. Joanna Nelson Rendón, "Ace the Interview," *Public Libraries Online*, May 8, 2014, http://publiclibrariesonline.org/2014/05/ace-the-interview/.

8. Joe Hardenbrook, "Library Interview Questions," Nailing the Library Interview, *Mr. Library Dude* (blog), accessed September 25, 2018, https://mrlibrarydude.wordpress.com/nailing-the-library-interview/library-interview-questions/.

9. Drexel University, "Sample Interview Questions," Steinbright Career Development Center, accessed December 6, 2018, https://drexel.edu/scdc/professional-pointers/interviewing/sample-interview-questions/.

10. Indiana Library Federation, "Career Center: Interview Questions," accessed December 6, 2018, https://www.ilfonline.org/networking/.

11. University of Washington, Information School, "Job Interviews: Frequently Asked Interview Questions," Advising and Support, accessed December 6, 2018, https://ischool.uw.edu/advising-support/career-services/interviews; and University of Washington, Information School, "Sample Interview Questions: LIS Specific and Generic," Google Doc, accessed December 6, 2018, https://docs.google.com/file/d/1g8fEGe0KoVrKwODXyvQButA7D4qRdG7oURhUxvou0lWtzG9QU7eFzjrA7xML/edit?hl=en&pli=1.

12. Nanako Kodaira, "Academic Interview Process," American Library Association, New Members Round Table, accessed December 6, 2018, http://www.ala.org/rt/nmrt/oversightgroups/comm/resreview/process.

13. University of North Carolina, University Library, "Sample Interview Questions," October 2014, "https://library.unc.edu/wp-content/uploads/2014/10/interview-questions.pdf.

14. Society for Human Resource Management, "Interview Questions," accessed July 4, 2018, https://www.shrm.org/ResourcesAndTools/tools-and-samples/interview-questions/Pages/default.aspx.

15. Adapted from Emily Weak, "*Hiring Librarians*' Library Interview Question 'Database,'" *Hiring Librarians* (blog), accessed September 25, 2018, http://tinyurl.com/InterviewQuestionsRepository.

16. Adapted from San José State University, "Behavioral Interview Questions."

17. Adapted from Hardenbrook, "Library Interview Questions."

18. Nicole Cavazos, "How to Rehearse for a Job Interview," ZipRecruiter (blog), accessed September 9, 2018, https://www.ziprecruiter.com/blog/how-to-rehearse-for-a-job-interview/.

BIBLIOGRAPHY

Bureau of Labor Statistics. "Occupational Outlook Handbook." Last modified April 13, 2018. https://www.bls.gov/ooh/.

Cavazos, Nicole. "How to Rehearse for a Job Interview." ZipRecruiter (blog). Accessed September 9, 2018. https://www.ziprecruiter.com/blog/how-to-rehearse-for-a-job-interview/.

Drexel University. "Sample Interview Questions." Steinbright Career Development Center. Accessed December 6, 2018. https://drexel.edu/scdc/professional-pointers/interviewing/sample-interview-questions/.

Florida State University Libraries. "Library and Technology Jobs: Library Interview Questions." Last updated May 5, 2017. http://guides.lib.fsu.edu/c.php?g=352933&p=2383379.

Hardenbrook, Joe. "Library Interview Questions." Nailing the Library Interview. *Mr. Library Dude* (blog). Accessed September 25, 2018. https://mrlibrarydude.wordpress.com/nailing-the-library-interview/library-interview-questions/.

Indiana Library Federation. "Career Center: Interview Questions." Accessed December 6, 2018. https://www.ilfonline.org/networking/.

Kodaira, Nanako. "Academic Interview Process." American Library Association, New Members Round Table. Accessed December 6, 2018. http://www.ala.org/rt/nmrt/oversightgroups/comm/resreview/process.

Lincoln, Ruth. "Conflict in the Job Interview: How to Approach the Tricky Questions." *INALJ*. October 4, 2013, and August 29, 2014. http://inalj.com/?p=42145.

McNally, Brad. "Behavioral Interviews (And How You Can Use Them to Your Advantage)." *INALJ*. April 7, 2014. http://inalj.com/?p=67484.

Minnis, Sarah. "Skills Matrix." University of Kentucky, Lewis Honors College. Accessed November 28, 2018. http://www.uky.edu/honors/sites/www.uky.edu.honors/files/Skills%20Matrix.pdf.

Nelson Rendón, Joanna. "Ace the Interview." *Public Libraries Online*. May 8, 2014. http://publiclibrariesonline.org/2014/05/ace-the-interview/.

San José State University, School of Information. "Behavioral Interview Questions." Accessed September 25, 2018. http://ischool.sjsu.edu/behavioral-interview-questions.

Society for Human Resource Management. "Interview Questions." Accessed July 4, 2018. https://www.shrm.org/ResourcesAndTools/tools-and-samples/interview-questions/Pages/default.aspx.

University of Illinois, College of Law Library. "LIS 530 GLE: Legal Resources: The Interview Process." Last updated December 4, 2018. https://libguides.law.illinois.edu/c.php?g=494760&p=3685748.

———. "Sample Interview Questions: LIS Specific and Generic." Google Doc. Accessed December 6, 2018. https://docs.google.com/file/d/1g8fEGe0KoVrKwODXyvQButA7D4qRdG7oURhUxvou0lWtzG9QU7eFzjrA7xML/edit?hl=en&pli=1.

University of North Carolina, University Library. "Sample Interview Questions." October 2014. "https://library.unc.edu/wp-content/uploads/2014/10/interview-questions.pdf.

University of Washington, Information School. "Job Interviews: Frequently Asked Questions." Advising and Support. Accessed December 6, 2018. https://ischool.uw.edu/advising-support/career-services/interviews.

———. "Sample Interview Questions: LIS Specific and Generic." Google Doc. Accessed December 6, 2018. https://docs.google.com/file/d/1g8fEGe0KoVrKwODXyvQButA7D4qRdG7oURhUxvou0lWtzG9QU7eFzjrA7xML/edit?hl=en&pli=1.

Weak, Emily. "*Hiring Librarians*' Library Interview Question 'Database.'" *Hiring Librarians* (blog). Accessed September 25, 2018. http://tinyurl.com/InterviewQuestionsRepository.

———. Search results for "Interview Questions Repository." *Hiring Librarians* (blog). Accessed December 6, 2018. https://hiringlibrarians.com/?s=Interview+Questions+Repository.

CHAPTER 5

Following the Interview

After the interview you should be prepared to do several follow-up activities. And then if you are offered the position you may even have more work ahead of you. This chapter will break down the self-reflection process, thank-you notes, the job offer, the art of negotiation, accepting the job, declining the job, and, finally, rejection.

SELF-REFLECTION

Once your interview is complete, it is essential to reflect on your performance—and not just your performance in the interview. You should reflect on the entire job-search process, paying particular attention to the position(s) where you received interviews. This section will provide some tips and information to use in reflecting on the interview and the entire application process.

Interview

As soon as you can following your interview, you should reflect on your performance during that interview. Think about what you did well and aspects you can improve in future interviews. Were there things you did not understand? These may be important aspects to consider. The list of questions below can help guide you in your self-reflection on the interview.

1. What do you think went well? Identify at least one thing you feel went well about the interview. Even if you feel the interview

was a complete failure, look for something, even very minute, that went well. By identifying things that went well you can help boost your confidence for future interviews and additional contact related to that interview.

2. What do you think you can improve on? Just as you should identify at least one thing that went well, you should also identify at least one thing you can improve upon. Even if the interview went excellently and you feel you did everything right, think about what you did least successfully and why. If you feel that nothing went right, then it might be best to concentrate on one to three things that seem the most promising for improvement and try to work on those.

3. What did you learn about yourself? Talking to someone else about yourself can be a great eye-opener. What did you learn about yourself besides what you did well and what you can improve upon? For example, did you find yourself talking exclusively about one previous position or one particular class? If so, this may indicate a genuine interest in that particular aspect of library or information work related to those experiences.

4. What questions do you still have? Sometimes an interview leaves you with new questions. Are those questions significant enough that you should follow up on them as they arise, or can the questions wait until you hear back following the interview?

5. What additional things did you learn about the job? In most interviews the interviewer(s) explain (even if just briefly) the job position. Did they reveal additional duties or responsibilities you were not aware of or do not feel comfortable doing? Did they ask questions that focused on those new aspects you were not prepared for? What does that reveal about the position itself or your feelings about the position?

6. What did you learn about the organization? Whether or not there was a formal presentation or introduction to the organization, you likely learned a great deal about the organization in the brief time of your interview. During the interview you may have noticed certain interviewers taking the lead. Or you may have noticed that the dynamic changed when the departmental supervisor was or was not present. These are just some examples of observations

or insights you may learn that may impact your desire for the position.

After answering questions five and six, you should take time to reflect on what this information reveals about the job and your interest in it.

Application Materials

After reflecting on the interview, you should go back to your application materials to see what changes or improvements you can make to these documents. For example, in answering a question during your interview you may have stumbled upon a skill, job duty, or area of knowledge that you may have not realized and/or included on your résumé thus far. This is a great time to add those additional pieces to your résumé if they would be relevant to other potential positions.

Additionally, the interviewer(s) may have asked questions about elements of your résumé. If so, you may want to consider clarifying or wording some things differently on your application materials or removing elements from your application materials.

THANK-YOU NOTES

Thank-you notes serve as a gesture of appreciation to those involved in the interview process. You should send a thank-you note or notes following any interview, whether it is an initial screening interview or the final interview. You should send a thank-you note to each person involved in the interview and possibly even the interview process. For example, if the library director is interviewing you, then you should send a thank-you note to the director. You should also consider sending a thank-you note to the human resources person or administrative assistant that scheduled the interview. After all, they invested significant time in making the interview possible. You should especially consider sending a thank-you to administrative staff when interviewing for an academic library position or any other interview where they arranged travel, hotel, or other accommodations. In an academic-library setting you may also want to send multiple thank-you notes to any significant faculty, staff, or students that participated or assisted in the interview, even if they did not actually formally interview you. For example, you may have been shuttled to and from the airport by a faculty or staff member. This person may provide input to the hiring committee based on this experience. Providing a thank-you note may be a good way to remind them of the positive interactions you shared. Even if things did not go well, sending a thank-you note may help change their impression of your interactions.

Thank-you notes can be handwritten or typed and can be delivered via regular mail or e-mail. Any format is acceptable, but there are certain things you should consider when selecting your preferred format:

1. How long before the interviewer makes a decision? Typically during the interview you will learn when a hiring decision will be made. If the decision will be made within forty-eight hours, you may need to send an e-mail thank-you to ensure the interviewer receives the note before making their final decision.[1] If the decision is to be made further out, it may be appropriate for you to send a handwritten note.
2. What type of job is it? If you are seeking technical positions, a handwritten note could be considered "irrelevant,"[2] but in other instances a handwritten note may show you took the extra time and effort to write a personal message.

No matter which format you choose, your thank-you note should contain some very specific components:

1. Thank the interviewer(s) for their time. Be specific by reminding them when you met with them.
2. Be sure to provide information or mention anything you indicated you would follow up on after the interview.
3. Remind them of how your interview stood out and why you are the best candidate. You can do this by highlighting a positive from the interview.
4. Offer to provide any additional information upon request.
5. Close with an acceptable and professional complimentary close (e.g., "Sincerely,") and your signature.

THE JOB OFFER

Once interviews have concluded and the candidates have been ranked, the library or library-related organization will contact the top candidate (you, hopefully), usually over the phone or via e-mail, to confirm you are still interested. If you are still interested, you can accept the offer as it is, or you can choose to negotiate. Before you do either, you should evaluate the job and the offer to see if both match your personal and professional needs and goals.

Evaluate the Job

When you evaluate the job, you should reflect on both the job description and what you learned and observed about the job during the interview.

Review the job description. Does it seem to match up with your impression after the interview? Is there any information about the duties or role in the offer? Below are some things to consider:

- *Job duties.* Do the job duties seem to align with what was discussed in the interview or job offer, or does the description seem radically different? If so, you should seek clarification (in writing, preferably) of the job duties.
- *Work hours.* Do the working hours match up with those listed in the job description? If not, confirm why. If working hours are not mentioned in the job description or job offer, then you should ask for clarification of expected hours.
- *Salary.* Does the salary or pay match that projected on the job description? If there is a discrepancy (either significantly higher or lower), you should seek clarification. A different salary could indicate a change in performance expectations (nonexempt to exempt) or a change in job rank (you could move from librarian to library assistant if lower salary or vice versa if higher).
- *Work location.* Does the location in the offer match that of the job description? If not, you should seek clarification. A different location may change the job expectations, coworkers, supervisor,

and expected cost of living, among other things. This may impact your desire or ability to accept the position.

Evaluate the Offer

When you evaluate the offer itself, you should consider salary, benefits, working conditions, start date, and any other pertinent criteria.

Salary

When considering salary, you need to consider whether it is competitive and whether it meets your minimum requirements. Glassdoor.com and the the Bureau of Labor Statistics' *Occupational Outlook Handbook* are examples of general resources you can use to learn about salary expectations for certain positions. Robert Half Technology produces an annual technology and IT salary guide that provides "starting salary ranges for nearly 80 jobs in the tech industry."[3] *Library Journal* recently published salary information obtained from its 2017 survey of graduates from forty of the fifty-two ALA–accredited LIS programs.[4] These are all great starting points to determining whether or not the proposed salary is competitive. There are other things you may need to consider that may not be reflected in these tools when evaluating the salary:

1. *Consider cost of living.* Remember, depending on the location of the job, things such as housing, transportation, taxes (state, local, property, and sales), etc., may be more costly.
2. *Consider whether the position is exempt or nonexempt.* What are other similar positions? Exempt positions are typically salaried, and you may be expected to work beyond the regularly scheduled hours.

It is equally important that you reflect on your own personal needs when considering salary. You definitely need to determine whether the salary is within the range of what you need to cover (e.g., living expenses, any residual school expenses, savings, etc.). When looking at that salary number, remember there are some other factors you may need to consider:

1. *Consider when you will get paid.* Many faculty and salaried positions are paid monthly, whereas some other library staff positions may be paid biweekly. There is no industry standard for the distribution of payment, so you should plan to check with the library or library-related organization regarding when payments are disbursed.
2. *Consider any regular deductions that may occur in pay, reducing the amount of take-home pay.* Standard deductions might include taxes, health benefits, and retirement benefits. Additional deductions may cover the cost of parking or uniforms. Sometimes these can be taken directly out of your check, and in other instances you may have to pay for these separately. Either way, they may impact your disposable income.

Benefits

Another very important consideration in the job offer is the benefits package. What types of benefits come with the position? The most common would be leave time and health and retirement benefits. Do you get vacation time? If so, how much, and when does it start accumulating? Are there any restricted times of year you cannot use your vacation? Do you get separate sick leave? If so, how does it accumulate?

FACULTY AND SCHOOL-LIBRARY PAYMENTS FOR NINE TO TWELVE MONTHS

Another aspect related to when you get paid is the frequency with which you get paid. There are some library and library-related positions that work only nine to eleven months per year. Library science teaching faculty and school-media specialists are the most common of these positions. If you are applying for one of these positions, you may also need to consider how your salary will be disbursed. Will it be divided across twelve months even though you won't work all twelve months, or will you be paid only during the months you work? This may not seem that significant for you, but you may want to confirm when your pay will be distributed, as you could be required to pay more in taxes or use credit cards or other forms of debt to cover expenses until you receive payment.

Some organizations have switched to a personal-day policy instead of separate sick and vacation days. It might be important to know this particular library or library-related organization's policy on leave time.

Health and retirement benefits are another important consideration related to compensation. Employers are now required to report employer contributions as part of an employee's total compensation package. You should confirm that the offered salary does not factor in the employer contributions for these things, but remember to factor in any mandatory or optional coverages in health care and retirement that is your financial responsibility.

Some less common but potentially still important additional benefits for you to consider may include on-site childcare, whether or not the job is pet friendly, casual dress, meal plans, employee discount, etc. For example, some larger employers like universities or global corporations may offer on-site childcare. The cost to use this service may be deducted from your pay, since not all employees would likely need this service, but the convenience of on-site care may be worth your financial obligation. If you are an animal lover or if you have extreme allergies then a pet policy may be a significant consideration for you. For example, if employees can bring their dogs to work but you have a severe allergy, then this may not be a good fit for you regardless of some of the other considerations. Casual dress and meal plans may also be benefits worth considering, because these could contribute to a better bottom line if you do not have to expend additional funds for these items. Finally, employee discounts can be a huge contributing factor for some. For example, many colleges or universities provide tuition discounts for employees' children. That is like getting a significant bonus if you have one or more children planning to go to college.

Working Conditions

Working conditions are another big consideration when evaluating the job. You may want to consider working hours, location, telework, and any other conditions pertinent to you. There are several working-hours matters you should consider when deciding whether to accept a position:

- You should consider any personal, educational, professional, and medical obligations you may have that could limit your ability to work the stated hours or any possible additional hours, such as overtime.
- You should consider and ask about any required dates or times you must work regularly. For example, does the public library you applied to require that everyone work the summer reading kickoff? If so, when is the event typically held? Does the academic library require that everyone work during midterms or finals' week? If so, what are the required hours? Are they the same as your normal working hours, or are they modified to meet the needs of the students? For example, libraries at Indiana University at Bloomington offer extended hours during the week of finals. Normally they are open until 12 a.m. through the week and 9 p.m. on Fridays and Saturdays; however, during finals' week the library remains open until 2 a.m. the entire week (including Fridays and Saturdays).[5]
- You should consider the availability of flex time. Are you required to work the exact hours of operation, or does it appear that you could alter your work hours to achieve an optimal work-life balance? For example, can you alter your daily schedule to drop off or pick up your child or pet from daycare?

You should consider a number of questions related to location when deciding whether or not to accept a position. What location would you be reporting to? Is this location reasonable for your commute? How would you travel to and from work? How long will your commute be? Will you need to report to multiple locations daily, weekly, etc.? How does this affect commute time and wear and tear on your personal vehicle?

Whether you want to work remotely or not, you may need to investigate the options and expectations of telework. For example, is there an option to work from home regularly or on an as-needed basis? More importantly, is there an expectation for you to work from home? Are you required to respond to e-mails when they arrive, address information needs any hour of the day, or be on-call remotely? Finally, whether telework is optional or expected, do you have the necessary technology to work remotely?

Start Date

While getting an offer that includes a start date may be very exciting, there are some things you may need to consider:

- You should confirm that the proposed start date matches appropriately with any requirements for notice at your current employer.
- You should make sure the proposed start date allows adequate time for you to relocate if a move is required for the new position.
- You should make sure the new start date still allows sufficient time to fulfill any professional or personal obligations you must keep. For example, if you have an obligation to present at a professional conference, can you still present at the conference if you start on the suggested date? If you are unsure, this may be a question you ask when negotiating the job.

Other Criteria

You may have additional considerations significant to your evaluation of the job offer. Be sure to think through each one before accepting a position. Remember, once you accept the position it is no longer possible to negotiate duties, salaries, benefits, or any other criteria.

THE ART OF NEGOTIATION

Once being offered a position you have the right to inquire or make suggestions about the position, salary, benefits, or other details before accepting or rejecting the position. Equally, the library or library-related organization has the right to request your response to the job offer without answering any questions or making any modifications to their offer. This means that before you try to negotiate you need to determine whether or not you are willing to accept the position as is and if not what the minimum is that you are willing to accept. Asking questions about the job or the offer may help clarify where you stand on the current offer.

Asking Questions

After you have evaluated the job and the offer, it is time to ask any follow-up questions related to your evaluation and negotiate if you are still interested in the position. Questions can be asked via e-mail, by phone call, or in person.

Your questions should focus on clarifying or seeking information to aid in your decision. This is not a time to ask questions just to be asking. However, it is certainly a time to address any questions that arose in your evaluation of the job or the job offer. You don't want to accept a job still having questions or concerns. Clarifying questions might include asking about the location, certain job responsibilities, or reporting structure in the library or library-related organization.

Negotiation Talks

If you plan to negotiate any part of the job offer, you should plan to negotiate after receiving the job offer (formal or informal) but before accepting the position. You should plan to negotiate over the phone or in person. You should avoid negotiating via e-mail.[6] You can always follow up via e-mail or in writing after any negotiation is finished to request the negotiated terms in writing.

The Graduate College at the University of Illinois suggests you do four things before you begin your negotiation talks: research, assess your leverage, prioritize and set goals, and plan the conversation.[7]

- *Research.* You should investigate the job duties, salaries, and benefits of similar positions in similar libraries or library-related organizations. You can share this information in your negotiation discussion.
    - You should collect and be ready to share salary information you collected when evaluating the job offer if you plan to negotiate salary.

- If you plan to negotiate job duties or other benefits (vacation, childcare, etc.), you need to find industry examples to support that what you are negotiating is the norm.
- You may also consider indirect factors (besides performance or position-based concerns) like cost of living or moving stipend and expenses. To negotiate these or similar indirect factors it is important to share accurate data based on location, since these factors may vary geographically.
- You should research more about yourself and what you can bring to the position. Be prepared to justify how the higher pay, different benefits, or other amenities you are seeking will pay off for the library or library-related organization. You might suggest a project or program you plan to implement or share an idea to save the library or library-related organization money or to improve their customer service. Either way, you want to focus on how your knowledge and experience are key to the suggestion.

- *Assess your leverage.* You can measure your leverage (the extent to which you have influence or power over the employer) based on time, competition, need, and desire.[8]
  - "Time" refers to how long you have or can take to make a decision. For example, if the library is trying to hire someone who can start right away to help them file e-rate paperwork, then you may have more negotiation power. They may be willing to accept your terms rather quickly so they can get you on board to share your expertise. However, if you were offered a faculty position that is not scheduled to start until the next fiscal year, your leverage may be reduced since the library or library-related organization would have more time to find a different suitable candidate.
  - "Competition" is based on the number of qualified candidates. This may be tricky to use as leverage since applicants rarely know how many other qualified candidates the library or library-related organization had. However, if you were able to distinguish yourself enough during your interview, through your application materials, and follow-up correspondence you might have some leverage. After all, the library or library-

related organization did offer you the job. The key is reminding them of that decision in the negotiation without sounding too assertive.
    - Your own "need and desire" can also factor into leverage. If you have multiple job offers you can use that as leverage to negotiation. If this is your dream library job you may feel as though you have less leverage because you are willing to settle to get the opportunity.
- *Prioritize and set goals.* You need to determine your most important negotiation criteria.
    - Decide before you begin negotiating what matters most to you (e.g., salary, start date, working hours, etc.).
    - Try to determine the least flexible criteria from the library-related organization's perspective.
    - You should try to focus on those that are your top priority but are more likely to be negotable from the library or library-related organization's perspective.
    - Be sure to define what your target goal is for each criterion.
        - Consider what the minimum is you will accept for any of the criteria you are negotiating.
        - Consider your ideal offer you want for each criterion.
    - You can create a chart to list each criterion, placing the current offer, your minimum acceptable, your ideal offer, other thoughts, and feedback for each. This will allow you easy reference during the negotiations. See the example chart in table 5.1 for an example. The feedback column is blank, but you would use this column to record counteroffers, comments, or other information you receive in the negotiations.
- *Plan the conversation.* Just as you planned and practiced for the interview, you should plan and practice to negotiate. Table 5.1 includes a thoughts column with some example thoughts you may consider and record. You can also include additional facts or information to share during the negotiations in this column. For example, if you reviewed the current salaries paid by the university library at the negotiating university or at another nearby university (many university salaries may be public if it is a publicly funded university) you should record this information and where you

Table 5.1. Negotiation Criteria

Criteria	Offer	Minimum Acceptable	Ideal Offer	Thoughts	Feedback
Salary	$32,500	$33,000	$34,500–$36,000	If the ideal offer cannot be met, then work hours, work location, or telework may help bridge the difference.	
Benefits (insurance, retirement, childcare, vacation, sick leave, etc.)	2 weeks of vacation after first year of service	Time off unpaid for already-arranged vacation	Earlier paid vacation time for previously scheduled family vacation	This must be worked out due to previously scheduled vacation.	
Work hours	8 a.m.–5 p.m.		7:30 a.m.–4:30 p.m.	This may be a negotiating option if salary is nonnegotiable.	
Work location	Home office	Home office, except branch location as needed	Branch location	This may be a negotiating option if salary is nonnegotiable.	
Telework	Not offered	None	2–3 days a week	This may be a negotiating option if salary is nonnegotiable.	
Start date	August 23	August 20 (two weeks' notice)	September 1	Ideally it would be nice to have more time to complete current projects with current employer.	

found the information. Then during the negotiation you will have quick access to information to help you decide whether to accept the counteroffer, reject it, propose a new counteroffer, or present a conditional acceptance. A conditional acceptance might be that you will accept the salary counteroffer upon successful negotiation of the hours, job duties, or some other aspect of the job. By placing this information on the chart and having a guide to reference, you should be more effective in your negotiations.

ACCEPTING THE JOB

Once you are satisfied with the offer, you should accept it. You can accept the offer in person, via e-mail, or over the phone, but ultimately you want a formal, written job offer that addresses and specifies negotiated terms. This document should include official signatures from the decisions makers (e.g., manager, library director, library board officials, etc.) and you, eventually (when you decide to accept). This document should include at least the salary and start date. You also want to confirm that it contains any negotiated terms. For example, if you negotiated an altered schedule to allow you to care for an aging parent or your spouse, you want the written job offer to include that altered work schedule (though the document does not have to include the rationale). This serves as confirmation and lessens the likelihood of issues with scheduling once in the position. This does not, however, mean that the library or library-related organization has to adhere to those hours for the duration of your employment. Once you determine the written offer is complete and you are satisfied, you should sign and return the offer.

After accepting your new position, you have several remaining tasks to accomplish before you leave your current position. The list below goes into more detail about each task:

1. *Giving notice.* You should plan to give at least two weeks' notice.
    - Check your current employer's staff or personnel manual to determine if more notice is needed. If so, you should give adequate notice, as your current supervisor or employer may serve as a future reference or professional partner.

- You should communicate directly to your supervisor.
  - You should try to set up a meeting with—or at least speak to—your direct supervisor to express your plans to vacate your current position. In this meeting you should avoid simply delivering or reading your resignation letter. Instead you should be sure to do each of the following:
    - Thank your supervisor for their time.
    - Share with them your good news about the new position (title and duties) and any contact information you already have for your new position.
    - Specify when you plan to start at your new position, and try to work with your supervisor to determine the best time for you to leave your current position.
    - Work with them to develop a plan for completing any current projects, distributing regular duties, etc. Discuss how you will use your remaining time and how to reassign your remaining duties.
  - You should deliver a written notice either during the meeting with your supervisor or shortly after. The written notice should be short and to the point but should include some important elements:
    - *Date.* You need to include a date on the letter to provide proof that you provided the required notice. This means that if your current employer requires two weeks' notice, then the date on the letter should be at least two weeks before the end date for your employment.
    - *Your name and employee ID number (if applicable).* You want to make certain that the written notice includes your name and employee ID number (if applicable) to make it easier for human resources or management to process and file your resignation.
    - *Last day of employment.* You want to include your official last day of affiliation with your current employer. This is mainly for personnel records and payroll but may also help your supervisor in reassigning your duties. If you plan to take vacation time during part of that leave, you need to coordinate this with your current supervisor and

determine whether the vacation leave should be included in the letter.
- *Contact information.* You want to provide your direct supervisor and human resources or payroll department updated contact information. If you are moving this may be especially critical to provide. Your current employer may need to follow up with you regarding separation benefits, outstanding projects, tax documents, etc.
- *New employer and position (optional but recommended).* You don't necessarily have to provide your current employer with details about the position you are accepting or the library or library-related organization, but it may benefit you and your new employer to do so.
  - Essentially, this information can serve as an invitation for future collaborations or sharing of information or resources.
  - Sharing your new information may also result in finding more connections you did not even realize you had.
- *Gratitude.* You should show some sense of gratitude to your current employer for the skills and experience you gained in your current position. Your gratitude should seem genuine even if your experience was not positive. You never know when your current supervisor or employer could reappear in your future professional life.
- You may need to deliver a copy of the written notice to human resources to be added to your official employee file.

2. *Wrap up work.* You should prioritize projects and duties in consultation with your supervisor and/or impacted coworkers before your last day at your current position.
   - Finish those projects and duties that you are able to finish with your supervisor's approval.
   - For those you cannot finish, your role should be more of a consultant.
     - You will likely need to meet with various employees to discuss the transition of duties.
     - You may even be asked to develop instructional guides or videos.

- You should cooperate with your supervisor to provide any assistance you can during your final days. You want to leave on a positive note.
3. *Contact references.* You should follow up with any references you provided during your interview process.
   - You should thank them for serving as a reference and also provide them with your new employment information.
   - It is important to maintain good relationships with references for your own professional relationships, but your new library or library-related employer may benefit from the connection as well. For example, if your new position is with a book publisher and one of your references works in a library or a library school you may want to connect the two since they may benefit one another.
4. *Get in touch with business contacts.* In addition to following up with your professional references you should consider following up with other connections you made in library school or previous employment that could be beneficial in your new role. For example, if you are accepting a job at an academic library and you interned or were a student worker at the same or a different academic library, you might reconnect with your former supervisor for tips or to see if you can meet to discuss your new opportunity.
   - You should follow up with certain outstanding applications.
     - You do not necessarily need to follow up with every outstanding application, but you should certainly follow up with any libraries or library-related organizations that have contacted you for an interview. It is professional and respectful and can help you stay connected with others in the library or library-related field. Below is an example of text you can use to withdraw from consideration for any position:

       Thank you for considering me for the _____ position. I recently accepted an offer to serve as _____ for _____ and would like to withdraw my application for the position in your library.

       I am including my contact information in the event we can collaborate on a project in the future.

5. *Update application materials.* You should update your résumé or curriculum vitae (CV) to signify the end of your current position and the start of your new position.
   - Even if you do not plan to apply for any new positions, it is still important to keep your résumé or CV current.
     - You may need to use it when applying for tenure or a promotion.
     - You may need to use it when seeking professional development opportunities.
   - Even if you do not know all the details of your new position, you should still add the position to your résumé or CV. You can certainly add details as you become more familiar with your new position.
6. *Update social media accounts.* If you include your employment information on social media, you should update your employer information.
   - You can end date your current employer and position as soon as possible.
   - You should plan to update your new employment information only once you officially start and confirm the hire went through.
   - You should get permission from the library or library-related organization before posting employment information online. Some organizations may have privacy or security restrictions that prohibit mentioning the company on personal social media.
   - If permitted to update, you may need to update employer, job title, location, dates of employment, etc., depending on the platform.

DECLINING THE JOB

There are a number of reasons you may decide to not accept a job offer. After an interview you may decide you are no longer interested in the job. Your negotiation attempt may go poorly. You may receive a counteroffer from your current employer. You may have a personal obligation that prevents your accepting the position. These are just some of the reasons you may need to decline an offer. No matter the reason, you need to make certain you want to decline the job. In most instances, once you decline an offer the library or library-related organization will extend that or a similar offer to the next qualified candidate.

When you are certain you do not want to pursue the offer, you should contact the library or library-related organization to officially notify them of your decision. It is important to contact them to project a sense of professionalism. While the library or library-related organization may not be pleased with your decision, following up means you are making an attempt to establish a professional relationship with the library or library-related organization. This may lead to opportunities for future collaboration or future employment with the library or library-related organization. Below are several examples of variations of text you might use in your message.

EXAMPLE 1

> Thank you for the job offer. At this time I must decline your offer. I have accepted another position to be the new _____ at _____
> Please keep my information on file in the event we can collaborate in the future (*or* for future positions that match my qualifications and requirements).

If you are declining the job offer because you cannot reach an agreement on salary, then you may elaborate on the fact briefly. You should still thank them for the opportunity.

EXAMPLE 2

> Thank you for the job offer. While I believe working for your organization would benefit both of us, I must decline your offer. Please keep my information on file in the event you have a future position that better matches my qualifications and salary requirements.

REJECTION

Now you are better prepared if you are offered a job, but what happens if you are rejected? This section will define rejection and discuss how you should handle it.

Defining Rejection

Your job search may not always end successfully. There are multiple ways you may encounter rejection from a potential employer:

1. You may complete the required application or submit the required application materials and never receive a response from a potential employer. This is sometimes the most challenging to deal with because you do not receive any information as to why you did not make it to the next step in the application process.
2. You may receive a rejection notice from an automated employment system. This typically happens if the automated system screens applicants based on predetermined criteria and you do not meet the minimum requirements.
3. You may receive a rejection notice from human resources or another administrative unit or individual. This rejection notice may arrive in lieu of an offer for an interview, or it may occur following the interview.
4. You may receive a rejection notice directly from the hiring committee or individual instead of an interview invitation or following an interview.

Responding to Rejection

Rejection can be hard to take, but your response to it may further impact your job-search process. You can make sure the impact is positive by developing a response strategy for dealing with rejection.

1. Read any rejection correspondence you receive. Be sure to look for any indications as to why you or your application materials were rejected. While many potential employers may not disclose specific details about your application and interview, there are some instances where the follow-up correspondence may indicate why you did not receive an offer.
    a. Sometimes the rejection is driven by external forces. For example, you may receive a rejection notice because the funding was cut for a position before a candidate could be offered the job.

b. Sometimes the rejection is driven by competition. For example, you may receive a rejection notice that indicates a more qualified or experienced candidate was selected.
2. Ask for clarification, especially if you receive a phone call from someone on the search committee. However, don't simply ask questions during the call. Ask about setting up a time to meet to see if you can get feedback on how you can improve your interview skills and your application materials. Not all searches and libraries or library-related organizations can or will accommodate this, but even one meeting from one rejection could tremendously improve your chances in your next interview or application.
3. Incorporate any feedback and applicable self-reflection (be sure to not be too hard on yourself) into future applications, interviews, and job searches.
4. Take inventory of your rejections. Document rejections you have received, and include any details as to why you were rejected. (This information can be added to the log from chapter 3.)
   a. Did you notice any patterns about the types of positions or library or library-related organizations that offered the rejections?
   b. Did you use any similar application materials for the rejected positions? If so, check for grammatical errors, incorrect information (e.g., an incorrect date for the length of a position worked), or other issue with your application materials?
   c. Did you find any correlation between the rejections and struggles in the interviews? For example, did you find yourself struggling with certain interview questions, the presentation, or another particular aspect of the interview process?

NOTES

1. Caroline Zaayer Kaufman, "Job Interview Thank You: Is It Better to Send a Letter or Email?" Advice, Monster, accessed October 21, 2018, https://www.monster.com/career-advice/article/interview-thank-you-email-letter.

2. Molly Triffin, "Interview Etiquette: Is the Handwritten Thank You Note Outdated?" June 9, 2014, https://www.forbes.com/sites/learnvest/2014/06/09/interview-etiquette-is-the-handwritten-thank-you-note-outdated/#52dd217314c9.

3. Robert Half International, "2019 Technology & IT Salary Guide," accessed September 23, 2018, https://www.roberthalf.com/salary-guide/technology.

4. Suzie Allard, "Placements & Salaries 2017: Librarians Everywhere," *Library Journal*, October 17, 2017, https://www.libraryjournal.com/?detailStory=librarians-everywhere.

5. Indiana University–Bloomington, "Libraries: Hours," accessed September 23, 2018, https://libraries.indiana.edu/wells/hours.

6. Gaia Vasiliver-Shamis, "6 Mistakes to Avoid When Negotiating Your Job Offer," *Inside Higher Ed*, April 23, 2018, https://www.insidehighered.com/advice/2018/04/23/how-negotiate-job-offer-effectively-opinion.

7. University of Illinois, Graduate College, "Getting Ready to Negotiate," Career Development, accessed July 26, 2018, https://grad.illinois.edu/careers/negot-prep.

8. Ibid.

BIBLIOGRAPHY

Allard, Suzie. "Placements & Salaries 2017: Librarians Everywhere." *Library Journal*. October 17, 2017. https://www.libraryjournal.com/?detailStory=librarians-everywhere.

Indiana University–Bloomington. "Libraries: Hours." Accessed September 23, 2018. https://libraries.indiana.edu/wells/hours.

Robert Half International. "2019 Technology & IT Salary Guide." Accessed September 23, 2018. https://www.roberthalf.com/salary-guide/technology.

Triffin, Molly. "Interview Etiquette: Is the Handwritten Thank You Note Outdated?" June 9, 2014. https://www.forbes.com/sites/learnvest/2014/06/09/interview-etiquette-is-the-handwritten-thank-you-note-outdated/#52dd217314c9.

University of Illinois, Graduate College. "Getting Ready to Negotiate." Career Development. Accessed July 26, 2018. https://grad.illinois.edu/careers/negot-prep.

Vasiliver-Shamis, Gaia. "6 Mistakes to Avoid When Negotiating Your Job Offer." *Inside Higher Ed*. April 23, 2018. https://www.insidehighered.com/advice/2018/04/23/how-negotiate-job-offer-effectively-opinion.

Zaayer Kaufman, Caroline. "Job Interview Thank You: Is It Better to Send a Letter or Email?" Advice. Monster. Accessed October 21, 2018. https://www.monster.com/career-advice/article/interview-thank-you-email-letter.

CHAPTER 6

Staying Relevant

As a library and information professional it is very important that you take an active role in your own professional development. The days of simply doing your job are in the past. There are several reasons you should plan to invest significant time, effort, and even money in your own professional development:

1. The Bureau of Labor Statistics reports that the average person changes jobs 11.9 times between the ages of eighteen and fifty.[1] Knowing this, and that your current position is likely not the last position you will ever hold, it is important that you invest in professional development to stay relevant and marketable in the library and information science industry.
2. The World Economic Forum describes the job market as a place of change, highlighting the potential for new job creation—the creation of jobs that did not even exist five or ten years ago.[2] You should prioritize professional development to stay aware of new and emerging technologies related to library and information science.
3. Your employer or potential employer may expect some level of professional development from you. In some cases—like with faculty at schools, for example—your employer may even provide professional-development or research funds to assist you.
4. Your position has state-, federal-, or governing-body-mandated certifications or licensure requirements.

a. Most states require professional public library staff to be certified. Some even require that paraprofessional staff be certified. (See the section on Professional or Technical Certifications below for more details.)
b. Some special libraries require other special licenses. For example, the American Association of Law Libraries reports that about 20 percent of law libraries, primarily law school libraries, require that their librarians hold a law degree.[3]

LIFELONG LEARNING

Early in your career you need to make a commitment to lifelong learning. College degrees and certificates, professional or technical certifications, and other professional-development opportunities are all ways to stay relevant and demonstrate to employers or potential employers your knowledge, skills, and dedication to the library or library-related profession.

Degrees and Certificates

While all library and library-related positions may not require a degree or certificate, obtaining one—or more—may lead to an increase in salary, promotion, addition of responsibilities, or receipt of other benefits. Regardless of whether you plan to study library science at all possible levels, it may benefit you to know the different options to determine which best suit your goals and current qualifications. Table 1.1 in chapter 1 suggests possible positions for some degree types, and the next section in this chapter provides more details about the four primary library and information science degrees.

> The field of librarianship has been tremendously impacted through the introduction of integrated library systems, electronic databases, e-books, and other technological advances. The introduction of the Electronic Resources and Libraries conference in 2006[4] is testament to the technology evolution taking place in libraries.

Associates' Degree and Undergraduate Certificate

The most basic type of college degree in library and information science is the associate's degree or undergraduate certificate. According to the American Library Association (ALA), there are at least twenty-nine library and information science–related associate degrees and approximately thirty-nine undergraduate-certificate programs in the United States and Canada.[5] Some of these programs are part of the Library Support Staff Certification sponsored by ALA. Students who attain an associate's degree or certificate in library or information science are prepared to be a library technician or other library paraprofessional. They take classes in information literacy, library technologies, technical services, and other library services.

Bachelor's Degree

If you have already earned an associate's degree or certificate or would just prefer to pursue a bachelor's degree, then a bachelor's in library or information science may be a good fit for you. ALA reports there are at least thirteen colleges and universities that offer the bachelor's degree.[6] Students who earn the bachelor's degree master skills in collecting, interpreting, and synthesizing information. Additionally, by earning a bachelor's in library and information science you have the credentials to step into many other information-based roles that require at least a bachelor's degree (e.g., database administration, market research).[7]

Master's Degree

The third and most popular type of library and information science degree is the master's degree. You can pursue a master's in library and information science after having earned a bachelor's degree. More institutions offer this type of library and information science degree than any other type of degree. The master's in library and information science is the standard in the library science profession. Most professional librarians are expected to have at least the master's in library science—the only level of library and information science degree that ALA certifies. Currently there are fifty-two ALA–accredited programs in the United States.[8]

PhD

If your interest in libraries extends beyond working in libraries and you are interested in researching or teaching others about libraries, then you may want to pursue a PhD in library and information science. While the Association of College and Research Libraries (ACRL) has affirmed the master's degree as "the appropriate terminal professional degree for academic librarians,"[9] many library and information science master's–granting institutions require a PhD to teach graduate (master's or PhD) courses. To learn more about library and information science PhD programs in your area or online, you can do a Google search for PhD programs, visit iSchools.org or ALA.org to see the lists of applicable programs, or question library staff and library science faculty in your master's program.

Professional or Technical Certifications

Depending on your position in a library or library-related organization, you may be required to obtain and maintain some kind of certification. And even if you are not required, you may consider obtaining an applicable certification. The following sections will review some professional and technical certifications appropriate for library and library-related professions. Keep in mind that the following information is primarily related to initial certification. Many of these certifications require you to earn continuing education credits to maintain your certification.

Library Certifications

Not all libraries require employees to obtain professional (or paraprofessional) certification, but many public libraries do require both professional librarians and paraprofessional staff to obtain certification once employed. Most K–12 public schools require their school-media specialist to receive a different type of certification through post-bachelor's certification.

There are two types of certifications that exist for public libraries: professional and paraprofessional certification. For public libraries that

> In the state of Kentucky, a professional librarian can become certified as a Professional I (the highest level) by simply having an ALA–accredited master's in library science. If the degree is not ALA–accredited, then the librarian would be certified as a Professional II.[10] Librarians in Kentucky must renew their certification every five years. To renew the certification, library directors must earn between seventy-five and one hundred contact hours (depending on the size of the library). An assistant director, a department head, or certain other designated library staff must earn fifty to seventy-five contact hours (depending on the position).[11]

require certification, you may be expected to meet the requirements for initial certification upon employment. The certification requirements may vary from state to state. You should visit your state library association's website for details about your state's certification program.

The ALA and the Allied Professional Association offer the Certified Public Library Administrator (CPLA) program. This is another certification option for public-library professionals with a master's in library science and at least three years of supervisory experience.[12] You would be required to complete one course in each of the following areas: budget and finance, management of technology, organization and personnel administration, and planning and management of buildings. In addition, you would be required to complete three elective courses from topics such as current issues, marketing, fundraising/grantsmanship, politics and partnerships, and serving diverse populations.[13]

The ALA and the Allied Professional Association offer the Library Support Staff Certification (LSSC) program for those who work in support positions in public libraries. The certification is based on three required competencies—foundations of library services, communications and teamwork, and technology—and seven elective competencies—access services, adult readers' advisory services, cataloging and classification, collections, reference and information services, supervision and management, or youth services—which can be met by taking associated classes or by preparing a portfolio.[14] You should visit http://www.ala-apa.org/lssc/ to learn more about this program.

In addition to holding a teaching certificate, many K–12 school-media specialists also hold a school-media certification. According to the American Association of School Librarians, qualified or certified school librarians have "been educated and certified to perform interlinked, interdisciplinary, and crosscutting roles as instruction leaders, program administrators, educators, collaborative partners, and information specialists."[15] "Certified" is the key word. You can earn your school-media specialist designation (certification) two different ways:

1. You can gain certification through a non-degree-granting school-media librarian K–12 certification program like that housed at Eastern Kentucky University (EKU). This certification requires the completion of twenty-four hours of coursework to satisfy the Rank 1 credential, but does not result in the attainment of a master's degree.[16] This means that you could work as a school-media specialist for any district that did not require you to have a master's degree, but your credentials would limit your ability to work in other professional library roles.
2. You can complete a master's in library science that has a school-media option. Simply completing a master's in library science will not allow you to work in a school-media-specialist role. You must enter a program that allows you to specialize in school media. EKU also provides a master's option with a school-media certificate. It requires the completion of thirty-three to thirty-six coursework hours.[17] The University of Kentucky is another school that offers a school-media-specialist option. The University of Kentucky master's is certified by the ALA. This means that should you elect to move away from school media you would also be eligible to work in some other types of libraries. Programs that are not certified by ALA may not provide the same transition between school and other libraries.

Library-Related Certifications

The previous section presented information about some different library certifications; however, those are not the only professional certifications applicable to library and information workers. Appendix 1 lists many library and library-related professional associations and indicates whether the association offers professional certifications or not. This list is not exhaustive, but it is a good starting point as you start to consider the value of professional certifications for you. Beyond that list in appendix 1—or in conjunction with it—you should also do the following:

1. Identify some of your top interests and talents as they relate to your professional goals. You should have learned a lot about your interests, talents, and employment in chapter 3. Focusing on your own interests, talents, and even previous employment may help you determine which professional certifications you should pursue. For example, if social media emerges as a consistent interest for you, consider a HootSuite certification.
2. Look through professional resources (publications, professional-organization websites, etc.) to determine what certifications the industry or profession prefers.
3. Explore your own network. Check with coworkers, mentors, and other colleagues to see what certifications they are seeking or are interested in pursuing. You or your organization may even benefit by sharing or reducing costs for multiple people in the same training. For example, the American Association of Law Libraries allows both individual and site registrations. The site registration costs slightly more, but it allows multiple people in one organization to participate in the webinar.[18]

Other Professional-Development Opportunities

In addition to degrees and certifications, many library- and information-related associations host professional-development events to help library and information professionals stay abreast of current issues and emerging technologies. You can find a variety of webinars, e-tutorials, association conferences, and in-person workshops and trainings related to your position or professional goals. You may even be able to gain continuing education credits (a requirement for many professional certifications) for your participation in these programs.

Webinars

Webinars are a feasible way for you to expand your knowledge and potentially gain continuing-education units (if required for your position, certification, or professional license). Webinars are typically one-time online sessions when one or more speakers present on a particular topic. Sessions are conducted virtually, using some sort of conferencing software such as Webex, Skype, or Zoom. Usually as an attendee you only need to meet minimum technology requirements to participate, like having a compatible browser and speakers on your computer. Usually the only interactive components are short polls and maybe a question-and-answer session, both of which can be done without a webcam or microphone.

While not all webinars are free, they do tend to be somewhat more affordable than most other professional-development opportunities, since you can participate from almost anywhere. There are a number of ways you can find both free and reasonably priced webinars:

1. Check your state library association's website for a professional-development association or calendar of training events.
2. Check all professional-association membership benefits. Some professional associations offer free or reduced prices to members.
3. Subscribe to LISTSERVs related to training or the particular training you seek.
4. Follow training, professional development, or library-related organizations on social media and check their websites.
5. Contact library vendors to see what types of training they offer for the products they support.
6. Connect with coworkers and other library contacts to see what types of training they have completed.

e-tutorials

Another feasible professional-development opportunity you can virtually participate in that expands your knowledge is an e-tutorial, which is slightly different from a webinar in that it covers a topic in more detail and requires that the participant be more involved. You may need to complete assignments, quizzes, or other tasks to demonstrate your understanding. Typically e-tutorials take place through some type of learning-management system (e.g., Blackboard Learn, Canvas, Moodle) and are led by college or university faculty or someone with extensive knowledge in the field.

Professional associations may offer e-tutorials (e.g., ALA, American Association of Law Libraries). You may also find e-tutorials through college and university websites. For example, you can find a number of different library-focused e-tutorials through Northern Kentucky University's Library Career Development Continuing Education webpage. These e-tutorials are instructor-led, eight-week sessions on topics such as foundations of library science, adult readers' advisory, youth services, library technology, supervision, teamwork, and collection management.[19]

Association Conferences

Most professional associations hold conferences to encourage collaboration among library and information professionals through the sharing of ideas about the industry, obtaining additional training, and networking with others in the industry and affiliated industries. These conferences may be held by state, regional, national, or international associations, and typically the attendance fee increases based on the level of the conference, as does the variety of topics and represented organizations.

If you have the opportunity to attend a conference, the benefits far outweigh the costs. There are several benefits to attending an association conference. While you may see similar benefits from webinars and e-tutorials, the benefits are typically intensified for professional-development conferences.

1. Your attendance—or even desire to attend—may demonstrate your dedication to the library field.
2. You may be able to count your attendance as continuing-education hours for a related certification.
3. You will increase your professional network.
4. You may return to your library or library-related organization with new techniques and ideas to implement. You will also likely

> **A NEW KIND OF CONFERENCE: THE LIBRARY COLLECTIVE**
>
> The Library Collective was established in 2015 by librarians for libraries with a goal of providing a platform to exchange ideas and build professional networks feasibly. The Library Collective is an independent, nonprofit organization that hosts an annual gathering. The annual gathering is different from your traditional association conference, focusing on active learning, partnerships, and practical knowledge at significant savings compared to many other professional library or library-related conferences.[20]

have contacts to whom you can reach out for questions and advise on implementing projects and developments in your own library or library-related organization.

The most obvious way to learn about association conferences is to visit the association's website. Many associations have conference or event pages on their websites. Most national associations also provide links to regional or state associations on their websites. You should be able to use this information to learn about regional or state conferences.

In-Person Trainings and Workshops

In-person trainings or workshops are decreasing in popularity due to tightening budgets and the growth and success of webinars and e-tutorials. However, if you have the financial support and time to get away, these are excellent ways to learn. In-person trainings and workshops are different than association conferences because in-person trainings and workshops typically refer to instructor-led, multi-hour, day-long or multi-day sessions devoted to extensive coverage of a particular topic. Pre- or post-conference trainings and workshops that occur before or after a designated conference would be considered in-person trainings or workshops because, even though they occur at a professional-development conference, they fit the definition above. Additionally, most conference registrations do not cover the costs of these pre- or post-conference workshops. You must pay additionally for these, making them optional as part of conference attendance.

You can find in-person workshops or trainings several different ways. As mentioned earlier, you can certainly find in-person workshops or trainings at many professional association conferences. Many professional conferences offer extensive pre- and post-conference workshops at additional costs. You may also be able to find in-person workshops and trainings through professional and technical certification websites and organizations. For example, the Kentucky Department for Libraries and Archives processes library certifications for Kentucky public libraries and hosts a continuing-education events calendar on its website.[21]

SHARING KNOWLEDGE

As a library and information professional or student you may have knowledge you can contribute to the library profession. This section will explore two primary ways to share your knowledge: presenting and writing.

Presenting

The first significant step to presenting is identifying professional associations related to your area of expertise. For example, if you are a teen or young-adult librarian, then the Young Adult Library Services Association (YALSA), part of the American Library Association (ALA), may be a significant group for you. You could submit a proposal to the ALA annual conference or ALA's Midwinter Meeting, or you could present at YALSA's Young Adult Services Symposium.[22] If young-adult services is not your area of expertise, you could consult the list of professional organizations in appendix 1 to research which host regional, state, national, and international conferences. You can visit the website of any specific professional organizations you are interested in to learn more about their conferences, presenter submission deadlines, and other important information.

Almost all conferences are open to association members to present and attend. Some may even accept presentation proposals from

> While working on a new program at the Scott County Public Library in Georgetown, Kentucky, the author submitted a proposal to the Library Informations Technology Associations (LITA) Mobile Computing Interest Group. She learned of the program through the LITA LISTSERV. The author's proposal on starting a device club was accepted, and she presented virtually in January 2015. Later she submitted a chapter for publication on the same topic, which was published in 2017.

nonmembers. Conference proposals are usually free to submit and are due anywhere from a few months to a year before the conference. Most professional associations solicit conference proposals through professional LISTSERVs, membership newsletters, the organization's website, word of mouth, social media, or other conferences.

Once you have identified some possible conferences, you should consider any identified themes, if provided, in the submission call. You should also consider whether you want to submit individually, with a colleague, or as part of a group (panel, poster, etc.).

After looking at the call for proposals and all the possibilities, you need to try to identify a particular topic. What about your own experience, knowledge, skills, and interests? Where do these things guide you? This may lead you to an obvious topic.

If reviewing your own experience, knowledge, skills, or interests does not lead to a topic, you are probably not alone. Here are some other things you can do to help narrow your topic.

1. Think about your own work. Often you have been doing something so long it seems mundane to you. Do you have a way to do a process or procedure in a library that is unique to your library or position? Did you start a new program in your library? Did you even try something and it failed? Sometimes failure can be life's greatest teacher.
2. Ask your coworkers or fellow students what topics matter to them.
3. Review questions asked and topics covered on related LISTSERVs. What does it seem those in the industry struggle with, have questions about, or show interest in? Does any of that match up with your own knowledge, skills, and interests?

4. Read the existing literature. See what is already out there on a topic. Can you take an interesting approach or perspective on something?

Writing a conference proposal—especially for the first time—can be intimidating. Below are some tips to help you write and submit your proposal.

1. Review programs for previous conferences to see what types of topics were covered. Also, notice what format was used in covering those topics. Most conference organizers strive to include variety in both the topics covered and the methods of presentation.
2. Seek advice and guidance from those within your library or library-related organization who have presented in the past. Even if they presented at a different conference from the one to which you are hoping to submit a presentation idea, they can likely give you some valuable tips.
3. Don't wait until the last minute to write a proposal. Seek submission requests early, and allow adequate time to write and review your proposal before submitting.
4. Allow time to proofread your submission. This sounds simple, but when there are so many submissions something as simple as imperfect grammar may get your proposal pushed aside. Think of submitting a proposal as a process as rigorous as applying for a job. Every detail matters.
5. Ask a colleague to review your work. Especially seek content and grammatical suggestions from them.
6. Follow the submission guidelines no matter how you feel about the guidelines. Most conferences receive more submissions than they can possibly host at sessions, posters, and other parts of the program, so decisions may come down to something as simple as which submissions followed correct procedures.

After you submit a proposal, there are a few things that might happen. The most immediate may be an on-screen confirmation (if you submit through an online form) or a confirmation e-mail. This confirmation may explain the process and wait time, or the confirmation may simply serve to confirm that your submission was collected. On very rare occasions, it may welcome you as a presenter; however, it is more likely that you will have to wait for a formal review process to commence before knowing whether your submission will be part of the program. The review process may happen as quickly as several days but may last a month or longer.

The review process may vary from conference to conference, but there are some similarities. Typically, once the submission window closes, all submissions will be gathered (usually electronically) and distributed to an appointed (or elected, in some cases) committee that will review and rank all of the submissions.

Once the review process concludes, one of two things typically happens. You receive notification that your proposal has been accepted, or you receive notification that your proposal has been rejected. Occasionally something different happens, and the review committee reaches out to see if you would be interested in joining a group of presenters on the same topic. Or they ask if you are interested in doing a poster presentation if they have already met their quota for presenters. If this happens, be flexible and willing to adapt your presentation format. Remember, any library-specific opportunities to share knowledge and skills are a plus for your résumé or CV.

If your proposal is accepted, celebrate in your success. The work will come later when you prepare your presentation. If your submission is not accepted, don't get upset just yet. Use this as a learning opportunity.

1. Investigate the response you received. Why was your proposal rejected? Is it something you can easily adapt or fix? Was the rejection based on the topic or the mechanics of the submission?
2. Follow up with the review committee if possible. Ask them how you can improve your submission for future submissions. Ask if there are other ways you can contribute to the conference. Volunteering at conferences also looks good on a résumé.
3. Apply the feedback you receive, and consider submitting to other similar conferences—after making any necessary tweaks, of course. For example, if you are a children's librarian or a school-media specialist, you may be able to submit the same topic or

proposal to the YALSA, the American Association of School Librarians, or even a smaller college or statewide conference.
4. Seek out others interested in the same topic, and try to revamp your presentation by incorporating information and examples from multiple libraries or multiple perspectives. You could apply next year (or to a different conference) as part of a panel or with multiple presenters.

Writing

Presenting at a conference is just one way to share your knowledge with others in the field. Another good way to share your knowledge and remain relevant is to contribute to the base of knowledge by writing or publishing. There are many ways you can contribute through writing. The section that follows will review some of the most popular ways to publish.

Blogging

Blogging is one of the easiest ways you can contribute to the library community. You can contribute by adding content to existing blogs, or you can create your own blog. There are benefits to either. The biggest

> The blog *INALJ* has been a premier source for library jobs since October 2010.[23] While it has undergone some changes over the years, its primary purpose remains the same: to help library students and librarians find library jobs. If you share this passion, *INALJ* seeks columns and individual pieces for publication.[24] Visit their site to learn about submission guidelines and see if they are currently accepting submissions. They occasionally seek content editors and managing editors.[25]
>
> TechSoup for Libraries is a nonprofit organization that administers a technology-donation program, offers free trainings for library staff, and produces a blog and newsletter that focus on a variety of technology topics of value to libraries. They actively seek content related to technology in libraries. Visit their webpage to see about publishing your "original, educational, and nonpromotional content about technology topics relevant to . . . libraries" at their blog.[26]

benefits for you to write for an existing blog would be to get experience, share ideas, and get recognition. The biggest benefit to the library community is your knowledge.

If you want to start by contributing to other blogs, there are some library-related blogs that regularly welcome contributions. Keep in mind that most are unpaid contributions, but writing for these blogs is a great way to get exposure and start a following.

If you choose to contribute to existing blogs, you should do the following before submitting any work:

1. Become familiar with the content on the blog before you submit.
    a. You want to make sure you are not duplicating content.
    b. You also want to make sure the content and topic are appropriate for the blog. For example, TechSoup for Libraries may not be interested in a post about an emerging job area for librarians, but *INALJ* or *Library Career People*[27] may be very interested in a piece about an emerging staff need in libraries.
2. Be sure to read and adhere to all the submission guidelines on the blog.
    a. Avoid submitting the same post to more than one blog. Proposing a topic to more than one blog may be acceptable as long as your post would be original for each blog.
3. Be sure to properly cite or seek appropriate permissions for any outside sources you include in your submission.
4. Be sure to proofread.

If you prefer to start your own blog, there are several things you should ask yourself before starting:

1. Are you technology savvy? While there are many tools to aid in your creation of a blog, you do still need to have some minimal technology skills. WordPress is probably one of the easiest and most user-friendly blogging platforms. Tumblr and Google's Blogger are other popular platforms, or if you are really tech-savvy you could create your own website to host your blog. No matter the format you select, you will want to be sure to include that additional skill set in your application materials.

2. Do you have a topic or issue that has enough depth and breadth to write about? Authoring a blog is different than contributing to an existing blog. You need an angle that allows for growth and expansion if you want to be successful.
3. Do you have time to devote to writing? Authoring a blog takes a consistent commitment over a substantial amount of time. Can you see yourself still dedicating time to the blog in six months? In a year? Beyond a year?
4. Do you have potential readers? Part of the success for blogs is the community following. Who would you invite to read your blog? Could they and would they contribute to the comments to keep the discussions going?
5. Do you have potential contributors? Some successful blogs utilize guest and contributing writers to maintain frequency of the blog posts.

After answering those questions, you should do a little more research before creating your blog:

1. You need to determine whether there is an information or communication need surrounding your topics and issues of interest. You may be able to determine this by asking colleagues or classmates, searching for existing blogs to identify gaps of coverage, following professional library associations on social media to look for current issues or events, and reading professional-development literature (e.g., *Public Libraries Magazine*, *College & Research Libraries News*).
2. You may want to interview some current or previous bloggers to learn more about the process and any technology glitches, information limitations, copyright issues, or other concerns that those bloggers encountered. The bloggers may also share writing tips and other ideas to help you get started.

Then before you start publishing your blog, you need to find your voice and your approach for the blog. *The Annoyed Librarian* is one of the most famous library blogs, which operated for over ten years as a standing column on the *Library Journal* website (but stopped creating new content in early 2018[28]). It was successful because it took a controversial approach to current topics in the library world. The author was bold and willing to address issues others wouldn't tackle. That voice contributed to the success of the blog.

Publishing

You may prefer to be published by a traditional publisher. There are four primary ways to get your knowledge published. First, you can submit pieces to professional or academic publications. Second, you can contribute chapters or essays to someone else's edited collection. Third, you can submit your own book proposal (as editor or author) to a publisher. Finally, you could self-publish. You should definitely include any of these on your résumé or CV.

Professional and academic publications are the two primary types of library and information science–related publications. Professional publications are typically produced by practitioners in the library and information science industry and may include white papers, conference proceedings, trade journals, bulletins, newsletters, and reports. Academic journals usually contain research and theoretical-based information, and many academic journals are peer-reviewed.

Since there is such a variety of professional publications, there is not one direct way to get published in a professional publication. There are several ways you could contribute to a professional library and information science–related publication:

1. You may be asked or required to contribute to a professional publication. For example, as an electronic-resources librarian your employer may need you to provide usage statistics and write a summative report for the annual report. If your library is testing a new technology product, you may be asked to write or contribute to a white paper used by marketers of the product.
2. You may present at an annual conference and have your presentation included in conference proceedings. For example, the NASIG (formerly the North American Serials Interest Group) publishes session and speaker papers and reporter summaries from its annual conference in *The Serials Librarian*.[29]

3. You can submit a proposal directly to a professional journal or bulletin. For example, the ALA accepts unsolicited manuscripts on "professional concerns and developments, . . . library-related legislation, and libraries around the country and the world" from various viewpoints and interpretations for publication in *American Libraries*, ALA's premier membership magazine.[30]
4. You can apply to be a book reviewer for publications like *Booklist*, the *Horn Book Guide*, *Kirkus Reviews*, or *Choice Reviews*. Each of these publications focuses on book reviews and has different criteria for reviewers. For example, since *Choice Reviews* is an ARCL publication for academic libraries, they require their reviewers to be faculty members or academic librarians with expertise a particular subject.[31]

Academic publications are a significant source for new trends in library and information science research and practices. Most library and information science faculty and faculty librarians are expected to submit to peer-reviewed academic journals, but they are not the only ones who can get published in a peer-reviewed academic journal. As a practitioner or a student you may be able to publish in an academic journal if you conduct theoretical or applied research related to library and information science.

In addition to publishing conference proceedings, *The Serials Librarian* publishes practical and theoretical articles on topics of interest to those working in serials, "collection development, acquisitions, cataloging/metadata, or information technology departments."[32] Topics may include publishing, purchasing, "peer review, cataloging, resource discovery or consortial developments" and other innovative topics related to scholarly resources.[33] Taylor and Francis publishes two volumes with four issues each year.[34] Each year one to two issues are dedicated to the conference proceedings, but the remaining issues contain a variety of articles, case studies, reports, essays, or book reviews. You can submit original, unpublished manuscripts on these or similar topics through ScholarOne Manuscripts, peer-review manuscript-submission software.[35]

Many academic journals have very strict submission guidelines. If you are considering submitting to an academic journal, you should review that particular academic journal's submission website and read all the guidelines or instructions. You will need to make sure you follow all requirements specified by that academic journal. Also, since many academic journals require that the submission be previously unpublished, you need to confirm the academic journal would be a platform for sharing your research. To determine this, you should review past issues of the academic journal and read information about the intended audience and topics covered in the academic journal.

Library and library-related edited collections are another way you can get published. These include essays, how-to guides, case studies, and practical examples authored by different library staff, librarians, library and information science students, or library and information science faculty and are grouped by topic or some other common element. Publishers and editors will typically work together to solicit contributions for an edited collection. You can find solicitations posted on social media, LISTSERVs, publisher websites, professional-association websites, or college and university websites. *A Library Writer's Blog*, *Library Juice*, *Academic Writing Librarians*, and *Dolores' List of CFPs* are blogs dedicated to sharing calls from publishers and editors for various types of publications.[36] And Primary Research Group Inc., for example, is one publisher regularly using the LITA LISTSERV to announce calls for writers for various surveys and monographs.

After you find one or more solicitations you are interested in pursuing, there are some important things you must consider:

1. Do you meet the stated requirements for authors?
2. Do you have expertise or experience in the particular topics being addressed in the edited collection?
3. Would you have time to write the piece by the specified deadline?
4. Do you plan to do the work yourself, or will you be working with one or more coauthors?

If you have extensive knowledge of or experience related to a particular library or information science topic, there may be an opportu-

> The author published her first piece "Public Library Summer Reading Registration on Google Forms" after seeing a call for submissions on the LITA LISTSERV.[37] Since that time she has had another chapter and an essay published as part of different collections. She learned of both of these collections through the LITA LISTERV. You could also find information on submissions at publishers' websites.

nity for you to propose your own book to a publisher. You can conduct research on your own to find a publisher focusing on the library and information science industry that is accepting solicited or unsolicited manuscripts. Or you can respond to a solicitation you see through a professional LISTSERV, social media feed, or other promotional method. Every year there are several publishers seeking new, emerging topics related to library and information science. Rowman & Littlefield, Libraries Unlimited, Library Juice Press, McFarland & Company, Neal-Schuman Publishers, and Emerald Group Publishing are just some of the publishers or imprints you could investigate if you are interested in publishing on library-related topics. You may also want to investigate different university presses to see if they are interested in publishing your work.

Another emerging way to contribute to the ever-increasing body of knowledge on library and information science is to self-publish. Just as you might start a blog because you see a gap in the existing literature, you could write a book and self-publish to fulfill a gap you see in existing literature and publishing solicitations. You could also choose to self-publish in the event your submission (either a proposal or a completed work) is not accepted by a publisher (but first confirm with the publisher that self-publishing is an option). If you are interested in pursuing self-publishing, the Westport Library in Westport, Connecticut, has a LibGuide with self-publishing resources to get you started.[38]

RECORD EVERYTHING

As you begin to expand your professional mark in the library and information science field, whether by earning degrees or certificates, attending and presenting at conferences, or publishing, you should record all the details. Record your educational accomplishments, key presentations you have made, any publications you have contributed to, etc. These details that may seem irrelevant at the time play a big role when compiling your cover letter and résumé or CV. It is especially important for faculty to include all professional development on their CV. See chapter 3 for more details on what information you should record.

NOTES

1. Bureau of Labor Statistics, "Number of Jobs Held, Labor Market Activity, and Earnings Growth among the Youngest Baby Boomers: Results from a Longitudinal Survey Summary," Economic News Release, United States Department of Labor, August 24, 2017, https://www.bls.gov/news.release/nlsoy.nr0.htm.

2. World Economic Forum, "The Future of Jobs: Employment, Skills and Workforce Strategy for the Fourth Industrial Revolution," January 2016, http://www3.weforum.org/docs/WEF_Future_of_Jobs.pdf.

3. American Association of Law Libraries. "Education: Become a Legal Information Professional," accessed August 12, 2018, https://www.aallnet.org/careers/about-the-profession/education/.

4. Electronic Resources and Libraries, "ER&L in a Snapshot," accessed September 21, 2018, https://www.electroniclibrarian.org/about/erl-in-a-snapshot/.

5. American Library Association, "Library Certificate and Degree Programs," accessed September 7, 2018, http://www.ala.org/aboutala/offices/library-certificate-and-degree-programs.

6. Ibid.

7. Best Colleges, "Best Online Bachelor's in Library Science Programs," accessed September 21, 2018, https://www.bestcolleges.com/features/top-online-library-science-programs/.

8. American Library Association, "Searchable DB of ALA Accredited Programs: Search Results," accessed September 7, 2018, http://www.ala.org/cfapps/lisdir/lisdir_search.cfm.

9. Association of College and Research Libraries, "Statement on the Terminal Professional Degree for Academic Librarians," accessed September 7, 2018, http://www.ala.org/acrl/standards/statementterminal.

10. Kentucky Department for Libraries and Archives, "Types and Requirements for Certification," Librarians: Library Staff Development: Certification

Program for Kentucky Public Libraries, last updated 2010, https://kdla.ky.gov/librarians/staffdevelopment/Documents/CertReq.pdf.

11. Kentucky Department for Libraries and Archives, "Kentucky State Board for the Certification of Librarians: Certification Manual 2017," Librarians: Library Staff Development: Certification Program for Kentucky Public Libraries, October 1, 2017, https://kdla.ky.gov/librarians/staffdevelopment/Documents/2017CertificationManual.pdf.

12. American Library Association–Allied Professional Association, "Certified Public Library Administrator Program," accessed August 12, 2018, http://ala-apa.org/certification/application/.

13. American Library Association–Allied Professional Association, "CPLA Program Standards," accessed September 7, 2018, http://ala-apa.org/certification/competencies-standards/.

14. American Library Association–Allied Professional Association, "Which Competency Set Should You Achieve?" Library Support Staff Certification: Getting Started, accessed September 7, 2018, http://ala-apa.org/lssc/getting-started/which-competency-set-should-you-achieve/.

15. American Association of School Librarians, "Common Beliefs," accessed August 12, 2018, https://standards.aasl.org/beliefs/.

16. Eastern Kentucky University, "School Media Librarian P-12 Certification Program," Library Science, accessed August 12, 2018, https://libraryscience.eku.edu/school-media-librarian-k-12-certification-program.

17. Eastern Kentucky University, "Master of Arts in Education—School Media Librarian," Library Science, accessed August 12, 2018, https://libraryscience.eku.edu/master-arts-education-emphasis-library-science#_ga=2.186398639.741576739.1534121671-631974144.1534121671.

18. American Association of Law Libraries, "Privacy & User Data Collection," September 27, 2018, https://www.aallnet.org/forms/meeting/MeetingFormPublic/view?id=98E00000002B.

19. Northern Kentucky University, "Workshop Schedules," Library Science Education Programs, accessed August 12, 2018, https://inside.nku.edu/libraryeducation/librarycareerdevelopment/workshops.html.

20. The Library Collective, "The Collective Annual Gathering," accessed August 12, 2018, http://www.thelibrarycollective.org/libcol/.

21. Kentucky Department for Libraries and Archives, "Continuing Education Events," accessed December 7, 2018, https://kdla.ky.gov/librarians/staffdevelopment/Pages/ContinuingEducationCalendar.aspx.

22. American Library Association, "Upcoming Annual Conferences and Midwinter Meetings," accessed December 7, 2018, http://www.ala.org/conferencesevents/upcoming-annual-conferences-midwinter-meetings; Young Adult

Library Services Association, "YALSA's 2018 Young Adult Services Symposium," accessed December 7, 2018, http://www.ala.org/yalsa/yasymposium.

23. Naomi House, "About *INALJ*," *INALJ*, accessed September 21, 2018, http://inalj.com/?page_id=10653.

24. Naomi House, "Write for *INALJ*," *INALJ*, accessed September 21, 2018, http://inalj.com/?page_id=65207.

25. Naomi House, "Volunteer at *INALJ*," *INALJ*, accessed September 21, 2018, http://inalj.com/?page_id=47338.

26. TechSoup Global, "Writing Guidelines for the Blog," accessed September 21, 2018, https://www.techsoup.org/writing-guidelines-for-blog.

27. Visit them at https://librarycareerpeople.com.

28. Annoyed Librarian, "End of the AL," *Library Journal*, March 29, 2018, https://lj.libraryjournal.com/blogs/annoyedlibrarian/2018/03/29/end-of-the-al/ (page no longer available).

29. NASIG, "Learn about NASIG: Publications," accessed August 18, 2018, https://nasig.wordpress.com/learn-about-nasig/publications/.

30. American Library Association, "Submissions," *American Libraries*, accessed August 18, 2018, https://americanlibrariesmagazine.org/submissions/.

31. American Library Association, "Information for Choice Reviewers," accessed August 18, 2018, http://www.ala.org/acrl/choice/reviewers.

32. Routledge, Taylor & Francis Group, "The Serials Librarian," accessed August 18, 2018, https://amo_hub_content.s3.amazonaws.com/Association92/files/Publications/WSER%20Nasig%20member%20rate.pdf.

33. Taylor & Francis Group, "*The Serials Librarian*: Aims and Scope," accessed August 18, 2018, https://www.tandfonline.com/action/journalInformation?show=aimsScope&journalCode=wser20.

34. Taylor and Francis Group, "*The Serials Librarian*: Journal Information," accessed August 19, 2018, https://www.tandfonline.com/action/journalInformation?show=aimScope&journalCode=wser20.

35. Taylor & Francis Group, "*The Serials Librarian*: Instructions for Authors," accessed August 18, 2018, https://www.tandfonline.com/action/authorSubmission?journalCode=wser20&page=instructions.

36. Visit http://librarywriting.blogspot.com/, http://libraryjuicepress.com/blog/, http://academicwritinglibrarian.blogspot.com/, and http://sites.psu.edu/doloreslistofcfps/.

37. Deloris J. Foxworth and Roseann H. Polashek, "Public Library Summer Reading Registration on Google Forms," in *The Complete Guide to Using Google in Libraries: Research, User Applications and Networking*, vol. 2, ed. Carol Smallwood, 133–44 (Lanham, MD: Rowman & Littlefield, 2015).

38. The Westport Library, "Self-Publishing Resources," last updated December 7, 2017, https://westportlibrary.libguides.com/Self-Publishing/Resources.

BIBLIOGRAPHY

American Association of Law Libraries. "Education: Become a Legal Information Professional." Accessed August 12, 2018. https://www.aallnet.org/careers/about-the-profession/education/.

———. "Privacy & User Data Collection." September 27, 2018. https://www.aallnet.org/forms/meeting/MeetingFormPublic/view?id=98E00000002B.

American Association of School Librarians. "Common Beliefs." Accessed August 12, 2018. https://standards.aasl.org/beliefs/.

American Library Association. "Information for Choice Reviewers." Accessed August 18, 2018. http://www.ala.org/acrl/choice/reviewers.

———. "Library Certificate and Degree Programs." Accessed September 7, 2018. http://www.ala.org/aboutala/offices/library-certificate-and-degree-programs.

———. "Searchable DB of ALA Accredited Programs: Search Results." Accessed September 7, 2018. http://www.ala.org/cfapps/lisdir/lisdir_search.cfm.

———. "Submissions." *American Libraries*. Accessed August 18, 2018. https://americanlibrariesmagazine.org/submissions/.

———. "Upcoming Annual Conferences and Midwinter Meetings." Accessed December 7, 2018, http://www.ala.org/conferencesevents/upcoming-annual-conferences-midwinter-meetings.

American Library Association–Allied Professional Association. "Certified Public Library Administrator Program." Accessed August 12, 2018. http://ala-apa.org/certification/application/.

———. "CPLA Program Standards." Accessed September 7, 2018. http://ala-apa.org/certification/competencies-standards/.

———. "Which Competency Set Should You Achieve?" Library Support Staff Certification: Getting Started. Accessed September 7, 2018. http://ala-apa.org/lssc/getting-started/which-competency-set-should-you-achieve/.

Annoyed Librarian. "End of the AL." *Library Journal*, March 29, 2018. https://lj.libraryjournal.com/blogs/annoyedlibrarian/2018/03/29/end-of-the-al/ (page no longer available).

Association of College and Research Libraries. "Statement on the Terminal Professional Degree for Academic Librarians." Accessed September 7, 2018. http://www.ala.org/acrl/standards/statementterminal.

Best Colleges. "Best Online Bachelor's in Library Science Programs." Accessed September 21, 2018. https://www.bestcolleges.com/features/top-online-library-science-programs/.

Bureau of Labor Statistics. "Number of Jobs Held, Labor Market Activity, and Earnings Growth among the Youngest Baby Boomers: Results from a Longitudinal Survey Summary." Economic News Release. United States Department of Labor. August 24, 2017. https://www.bls.gov/news.release/nlsoy.nr0.htm.

Eastern Kentucky University. "Master of Arts in Education—School Media Librarian." Library Science. Accessed August 12, 2018. https://libraryscience.eku.edu/master-arts-education-emphasis-library-science#_ga=2.186398639.741576739.1534121671-631974144.1534121671.

———. "School Media Librarian P-12 Certification Program." Library Science. Accessed August 12, 2018. https://libraryscience.eku.edu/school-media-librarian-k-12-certification-program.

Electronic Resources and Libraries. "ER&L in a Snapshot." Accessed September 21, 2018. https://www.electroniclibrarian.org/about/erl-in-a-snapshot/.

Foxworth, Deloris J., and Roseann H. Polashek. "Public Library Summer Reading Registration on Google Forms." In *The Complete Guide to Using Google in Libraries: Research, User Applications and Networking*, vol. 2, edited by Carol Smallwood, 133–44. Lanham, MD: Rowman & Littlefield, 2015.

House, Naomi. "About *INALJ*." *INALJ*. Accessed September 21, 2018. http://inalj.com/?page_id=10653.

———. "Volunteer at *INALJ*." *INALJ*. Accessed September 21, 2018. http://inalj.com/?page_id=47338.

———. "Write for *INALJ*." *INALJ*. Accessed September 21, 2018. http://inalj.com/?page_id=65207.

Kentucky Department for Libraries and Archives. "Continuing Education Events." Accessed December 7, 2018. https://kdla.ky.gov/librarians/staffdevelopment/Pages/ContinuingEducationCalendar.aspx.

———. "Kentucky State Board for the Certification of Librarians: Certification Manual 2017." Librarians: Library Staff Development: Certification Program for Kentucky Public Libraries. October 1, 2017. https://kdla.ky.gov/librarians/staffdevelopment/Documents/2017CertificationManual.pdf.

———. "Types and Requirements for Certification." Librarians: Library Staff Development: Certification Program for Kentucky Public Libraries. Last updated 2010. https://kdla.ky.gov/librarians/staffdevelopment/Documents/CertReq.pdf.

The Library Collective. "The Collective Annual Gathering." Accessed August 12, 2018. http://www.thelibrarycollective.org/libcol/.

NASIG. "Learn about NASIG: Publications." Accessed August 18, 2018. https://nasig.wordpress.com/learn-about-nasig/publications/.

Northern Kentucky University. "Workshop Schedules." Library Science Education Programs. Accessed August 12, 2018. https://inside.nku.edu/libraryeducation/librarycareerdevelopment/workshops.html.

Routledge, Taylor & Francis Group. "The Serials Librarian." Accessed August 18, 2018. https://amo_hub_content.s3.amazonaws.com/Association92/files/Publications/WSER%20Nasig%20member%20rate.pdf.

Taylor & Francis Group. "*The Serials Librarian*: Aims and Scope." Accessed August 18, 2018. https://www.tandfonline.com/action/journalInformation?show=aimsScope&journalCode=wser20.

———. "*The Serials Librarian*: Instructions for Authors," accessed August 18, 2018, https://www.tandfonline.com/action/authorSubmission?journalCode=wser20&page=instructions.

———. "*The Serials Librarian*: Journal Information." Accessed August 19, 2018. https://www.tandfonline.com/action/journalInformation?show=aimScope&journalCode=wser20.

TechSoup Global. "Writing Guidelines for the Blog." Accessed September 21, 2018. https://www.techsoup.org/writing-guidelines-for-blog.

World Economic Forum. "The Future of Jobs: Employment, Skills and Workforce Strategy for the Fourth Industrial Revolution." January 2016. http://www3.weforum.org/docs/WEF_Future_of_Jobs.pdf.

Young Adult Library Services Association. "YALSA's 2018 Young Adult Services Symposium." Accessed December 7, 2018. http://www.ala.org/yalsa/yasymposium.

APPENDIX 1

Professional Associations

Below is a list of many professional-development associations that may be of interest to you as a library and information science professional. This is by no means an exhaustive list, but it does reflect the magnitude and type of professional associations available to those in this field. In this particular list you will find the professional association's web address as well as information about available services.

Key: *The association has a job board. ^The association has a LIST-SERV. ~The association has a certification program.

- American Association of Law Libraries, *^ https://www.aallnet.org/
- American Association of School Librarians, http://www.ala.org/aasl/
- American Health Information Management Association, *~ http://www.ahima.org/
- American Indian Library Association, https://ailanet.org/
- American Library Association, *^ http://www.ala.org
- American Society for Indexing, ^ https://www.asindexing.org
- American Theological Library Association, *^ https://www.atla.com/Pages/default.aspx
- ARMA, *~ https://www.arma.org/default.aspx
- Art Libraries Society of North America, *^ https://www.arlisna.org/
- Asian Pacific American Librarians Association, http://www.apalaweb.org/

- Association for Computing Machinery, *^ http://www.acm.org
- Association for Information Science and Technology, *^ https://www.asist.org/
- Association for Institutional Research, * http://www.airweb.org/pages/default.aspx
- Association for Intelligent Information Management, *~ https://www.aiim.org/
- Association for Library Collections & Technical Services, ^ http://www.ala.org/alcts/
- Association for Library Service to Children, ^ http://www.ala.org/alsc/
- Association of American Publishers, * https://publishers.org
- Association of Christian Librarians, *^ http://www.acl.org/
- Association of College and Research Libraries, *^ http://www.ala.org/acrl/
- Association of Independent Information Professionals, ^ https://www.aiip.org/
- Association of Information Technology Professionals, * https://www.aitp.org
- Association of Jewish Libraries, ^ https://jewishlibraries.org/
- Association of Public Data Users, http://apdu.org/
- Association of Specialized, Government & Cooperative Library Agencies, ^ http://www.ala.org/asgcla/
- Black Caucus of the American Library Association, * http://www.bcala.org
- Black Data Processing Associates, * https://www.bdpa.org/
- Catholic Library Association, * https://cathla.org/
- Chinese American Librarians Association, *^ http://www.cala-web.org/
- Data Governance Professionals Organization, ^ https://dgpo.org/
- Digital Analytics Association, *^~ https://www.digitalanalyticsassociation.org/
- Independent Book Pulishers Association, ^ http://www.ibpa-online.org/
- The Library and Information Technology Association, *^ http://www.ala.org/lita/

- Library Leadership & Management Association, ^ http://www.ala.org/llama/about/join
- Medical Library Association, *^~ https://www.mlanet.org/
- Music Library Association, *^ https://www.musiclibraryassoc.org/
- NASIG, *^ http://www.nasig.org/
- National Association of Government Archives & Records Administrators, *^ https://www.nagara.org/
- National Association of Health Data Organizations, * https://www.nahdo.org/
- Polish American Librarians Association, https://palalib.org/
- Public Library Association, ^ http://www.ala.org/pla/
- Reference and User Services Association, ^ http://www.ala.org/rusa/
- REFORMA: The National Association to Promote Library and Information Services to Latinos and the Spanish-Speaking, * http://www.reforma.org/
- Special Libraries Association, *^ https://www.sla.org/
- Substance Abuse Librarians Information Specialists, ^ http://www.salis.org/
- Theatre Library Association, ^ http://www.tla-online.org/
- United States Agricultural Information Network, ^ https://usain.org/
- Young Adult Library Services Association, ^ http://www.ala.org/yalsa/

APPENDIX 2

Sample Résumé and Curriculum Vitae

Appendix 2

Sample Résumé and Curriculum Vita

Deloris Jackson Foxworth

Street Address
City, State Zip
Phone Number
E-mail

PREVIOUS BLOG (author): http://dfoxworth.blogspot.com/

TEACHING EXPERIENCE

Aug 2011–Present **Part-time Faculty**, Eastern Kentucky University
teach Introduction to Human Communication

Aug 2007–July 2010 **Visiting Professor,** Kentucky State University
teach 5 classes per semester, serve on committee and teaching team,
participate in Faculty Incentive Program for online course development,
develop teaching schedules, co-advise National Communication Association student club

July 2006–Dec 2006 **Adjunct Faculty**, Northwood University, Toyota Program Center
teach Principles of Marketing, Public Relations

Jan 2006–May 2006 **Part-time Faculty**, Jefferson Community College
teach Interpersonal Communications—online

Sept 2004–Mar 2005 **Part-time Faculty**, National College of Business & Technology
teach Introduction to Keyboarding, Public Speaking

TECHNOLOGY EXPERIENCE

Mar 2011–Present **Staff Assistant**, IRJCI, University of Kentucky
edit and write blog items, maintain website, make copies, perform general office duties

Oct 2005–Aug 2007 **Website Coordinator**, Georgetown News-Graphic
maintain website, design ads for newspaper, shopper, and internet,
generate website reports, create electronic tear sheets, make PDF archives

June 2001–Oct 2005 **Manager of Advertising and Communications**, Owen Electric Cooperative
maintain website, edit monthly newsletter and bill insert, create marketing reports for
board and employees, research and maintain knowledge base system, administer
community programs, coordinate annual membership meeting, represent Owen Electric
in community and regional organizations, assist with employee training

LIBRARY EXPERIENCE

May 2010–Nov 2010 **Library Student Worker**, Lexington Theological Seminary
update/enter records, answer phones, assist patrons at circulation desk, reshelf books,
conduct inventory

EDUCATION

June 2008–May 2010 Master of Science in Library Science, University of Kentucky

July 2000–Dec 2001 Master of Arts in Communication, Western Kentucky University

Aug 1995–Dec 1998 Bachelor of Arts in Business Administration, Kentucky State University

DELORIS J. FOXWORTH

Street Address, City, State 12345 | 123-456-7890 | first.last@email.com

EDUCATION

Western Kentucky University, Bowling Green, KY
Graduate Certificate in Career Services — 2018

University of Kentucky, Lexington, KY
Master of Science Library Science — 2010

Western Kentucky University, Bowling Green, KY
Master of Arts in Communication — 2001

Kentucky State University, Frankfort, KY
Bachelor of Arts in Business Administration — 1998
Specialization: Marketing

AWARDS

Graduate Assistantship, Western Kentucky University — August 2000–June 2001
Designed promotional materials. Conducted research. Substituted for faculty.

FACULTY EXPERIENCE

University of Kentucky, Lexington, KY
Part-time Instructor — School of Information Science — January 2017–Present
Taught online sections of ICT/IS 201. Scheduled to teach ICT/IS 202 in Spring 2019.

University of Kentucky, Lexington, KY
Lecturer — School of Information Science — April 2014–December 2016
Developed and currently teaching ICT 150 Experience ICT for UK Core, Inquiry in the Social Sciences. Taught ICT 200 Information Literacy and Critical Thinking, online and face-to-face. Coordinated ICT 596 ICT Internship and consulted with students about literature review. Advised majors, minors and graduate students. Served as faculty advisor for student association. Recruited students. Built ICT course schedules.

Eastern Kentucky University, Richmond, KY
Part-time Faculty — Communication Studies — July 2011–July 2012
Taught on-campus CMS 100 Introduction to Human Communication.

Kentucky State University, Frankfort, KY
Visiting Instructor — Communication & Theater — August 2007–July 2010
Taught SPE 103 Interpersonal Communication online and face-to-face. Developed and taught SPE 302 Interracial and Intercultural Communication and SPE 310 Persuasive Speaking. Served on "Academics with Attitude" quality enhancement plan teaching team. Participated in Faculty Incentive Program for online course development. Developed departmental teaching schedules. Co-advised student communication organization. Advised Speech minors. Recommended new communication titles to library based on allotted budget.

Northwood University, Georgetown, KY
Adjunct Faculty — Toyota Program Center — July 2006–December 2006
Taught and developed Principles of Marketing and Public Relations courses.

Jefferson Community College, Louisville, KY
Part-time Faculty — Online Instruction — January 2006–December 2006
Taught Interpersonal Communications using the Angel platform.

National College of Business & Technology, Lexington, KY
Part-time Faculty — September 2004–May 2005
Taught Introduction to Keyboarding and Public Speaking.

Jefferson Community College, Carrollton, KY January 2003–May 2003
Part-time Faculty
Taught Public Speaking.

Sullivan University, Lexington, KY September 2002–March 2003
Part-time Faculty
Taught Public Speaking.

LIBRARY EXPERIENCE

Scott County Public Library, Georgetown, KY
Technology Manager March 2012–March 2014
Developed and executed 3-year technology management plan. Applied for and processed e-rate funding application. Maintained library's social media presence.

Lexington Theological Seminary, Lexington, KY
Student Worker May 2010–November 2010
Assisted patrons with directional and reference questions. Reshelf books. Conducted inventory. Updated/entered records.

ADDITIONAL WORK EXPERIENCE

College of Communication and Information, UK
Staff Assistant January 2017–Present
Advised over 250 students in five majors. Connected students to campus resources. Coordinated Internship Information Session each semester.

Institute for Rural Journalism and Community Issues, UK
Staff Assistant March 2011–February 2012
Edited and wrote for the Rural Blog. Maintained Institute's website. Updated donation records.

Georgetown News-Graphic, Georgetown, KY
Website Coordinator October 2005–August 2007
Maintained website, designed ads for print and online, generated reports.

Owen Electric Cooperative, Owenton, KY
Manager of Advertising and Communications June 2001–October 2005
Edited monthly newsletter and bill insert. Maintained website. Created marketing reports for board and students. Researched, maintained, and administered knowledge management system. Administer the Owen Electric Scholarship program and the Washington Youth Tour.

Georgetown News-Graphic, Georgetown, KY
Graphic Designer February 2000–June 2000
Designed ads for the Scott Shopper and Georgetown News-Graphic.

PUBLICATIONS

Foxworth, D. (2018). Empowerment, teamwork and personal growth. In J. Brandon, S. Ladenson, & K. Sattler (Eds.), *Women in Library Information Technology*. Library Juice Press.

Foxworth, D. (2017). Starting a Device Club. In C. Smallwood (Ed.), *Technology Use Instruction in Libraries for Staff, Patrons, and Students*. McFarland & Company, Inc. Publishers.

Foxworth, D. & Polashek, R. (2015). Public Library Summer Reading Registration on Google Forms. In C. Smallwood (Ed.), *The Complete Guide to Using Google in Libraries Volume 2: Research, User Applications, and Networking*. Lanham, MD: Rowman & Littlefield.

PRESENTATIONS

LITA Mobile Interest Group, Virtual
Webinar Presentation 2015
Starting a device club during enhancing library instruction with mobile devices.

Kentucky Public Library Association
Panel Presentation 2014
Tracking Wi-Fi

Kentucky Communication Association Annual Conference
Great Ideas for Teaching Speech (GIFTS) 2009
Impromptu Preparedness

Western Kentucky University
Graduate School Forum 2001
Attack on America

MEMBERSHIPS – PROFESSIONAL ASSOCIATIONS

Kentucky Library Association	June 2012–June 2016
• Information and Technology Round Table Chair	September 2014–2015
• Information and Technology Round Table Chair-Elect	September 2013–2014
American Library Association	April 2012–2014
Kentucky Communication Association	April 2009–2010
World Communication Association	December 2008–2009

COMMITTEE ASSIGNMENT

Member, ICT departmental curriculum committee	August 2016–December 2016
Member, School of Information Science faculty search	April 2015–December 2016
Member, ICT departmental assessment committee	August 2015–May 2016
Member, School of Information Science curriculum committee	April 2014–December 2016
Member, College of Communication and Information retention committee	August 2014–December 2016

APPENDIX 3

Sample Cover Letter

Appendix 3

Sample Cover Letter

Deloris Jackson Foxworth

Street Address
City, State Zip
Phone Number
E-mail

June 19, 2010

Library Director
**** County Public Library
Street
City, ST 00000

Dear Director,

I am writing to express my interest in the Children's/Young Adult Librarian position at the **** County Public Library. I learned of the opening on KDLA's website and I wanted to contact you to express my interest in the position and specifically address my qualifications for the Children's/Young Adult Librarian position at the **** County Public Library.

In May, I completed all the coursework for my Masters in Library Science at the University of Kentucky. During the program my major interests outside the core requirements for the degree were children's literature and technology. The children's literature classes I completed include an introduction to children's and young adult literature, programming, and multicultural literature. Through these classes I had to read and write evaluations for numerous children's and young adult books. I had to develop story time programs, book talk programs, a collection development project and much more. In the technology classes I completed I learned about databases, social media, web design, and other emerging technologies impacting libraries.

In addition to the many hands-on projects I completed in the Masters in Library Science at the University of Kentucky, I can also bring knowledge of planning and organizing events and programs from my experience at Owen Electric Cooperative. Before completing my first Master's degree in Communication, I began working at Owen Electric Cooperative as Manager of Advertising and Communications. During the four years I worked in that position I was responsible for the external communications of the cooperative. A significant portion of my time was devoted to community programs. I was responsible for administering and scheduling the environmental education program, scholarship program, Washington Youth Tour program, and other community programs. In addition to these programs, I was the primary organizer for the Annual Membership meeting. I was responsible for coordinating employee volunteers and vendors, ordering supplies, and promoting the event.

It is my hope that after reading this letter and reviewing the enclosed resume you will consider me for the Children's/Young Adult Librarian position available at the **** County Public Library. I know I do not have the one year of preferred library experience however I have been working part-time at the Lexington Theological Seminary Library since May. In addition I know I can provide the library strong leadership in planning, organizing and implementing community programs. If given the opportunity to work with the children's and young adult department at the **** County Public Library I know I can use my knowledge and experience combined with the current library staff to carry on the wonderful programs already in place and develop many new and exciting programs for the library and its users.

I have enclosed my resume which provides an overview of my education and employment. Please look over it and contact me at your earliest convenience to schedule an interview. You can reach me on my cell phone at 000-000-0000 or via e-mail at *****@bellsouth.net. I look forward to having the opportunity to speak to you about my future contributions to the **** County Public Library as Children's/Young Adult Librarian.

Sincerely,

Deloris J. Foxworth

Bibliography

AIM Library & Information Staffing. "About AIM." Accessed June 24, 2018. https://www.aimusa.com/mission.php.

———. "Application Form." Accessed June 24, 2018. https://www.aimusa.com/app.php.

Allard, Suzie. "Placements & Salaries 2017: Librarians Everywhere." *Library Journal*. October 17, 2017. https://www.libraryjournal.com/?detailStory=librarians-everywhere.

American Association of Law Libraries. "Education: Become a Legal Information Professional." Accessed August 12, 2018. https://www.aallnet.org/careers/about-the-profession/education/.

———. "Privacy & User Data Collection." September 27, 2018. https://www.aallnet.org/forms/meeting/MeetingFormPublic/view?id=98E00000002B.

American Association of School Librarians. "Common Beliefs." Accessed August 12, 2018. https://standards.aasl.org/beliefs/.

American Library Association. "Information for Choice Reviewers." Accessed August 18, 2018. http://www.ala.org/acrl/choice/reviewers.

———. "Library Certificate and Degree Programs." Accessed September 7, 2018. http://www.ala.org/aboutala/offices/library-certificate-and-degree-programs.

———. "Searchable DB of ALA Accredited Programs: Search Results." Accessed September 7, 2018. http://www.ala.org/cfapps/lisdir/lisdir_search.cfm.

———. "Submissions." *American Libraries*. Accessed August 18, 2018. https://americanlibrariesmagazine.org/submissions/.

———. "Upcoming Annual Conferences and Midwinter Meetings." Accessed December 7, 2018, http://www.ala.org/conferencesevents/upcoming-annual-conferences-midwinter-meetings.

American Library Association–Allied Professional Association. "Certified Public Library Administrator Program." Accessed August 12, 2018. http://ala-apa.org/certification/application/.
———. "CPLA Program Standards." Accessed September 7, 2018. http://ala-apa.org/certification/competencies-standards/.
———. "Which Competency Set Should You Achieve?" Library Support Staff Certification: Getting Started. Accessed September 7, 2018. http://ala-apa.org/lssc/getting-started/which-competency-set-should-you-achieve/.
American Theological Library Association. "Library Director and Media Services." Accessed October 14, 2018. https://webcache.googleusercontent.com/search?q=cache:IIB5liwMUBMJ:https://www.atla.com/Members/development/jobs/Pages/Library-Director.aspx+&cd=2&hl=en&ct=clnk&gl=us&client=safari.
Annoyed Librarian. "End of the AL." *Library Journal*, March 29, 2018. https://lj.libraryjournal.com/blogs/annoyedlibrarian/2018/03/29/end-of-the-al/.
Association for Information Science and Technology. "Job Descriptions." Accessed December 6, 2018. https://www.asist.org/careers/occupational-paths/job-descriptions/.
———. "Occupational Paths." Accessed July 7, 2018. https://www.asist.org/careers/occupational-paths/.
Association of College and Research Libraries. "Statement on the Terminal Professional Degree for Academic Librarians." Accessed September 7, 2018. http://www.ala.org/acrl/standards/statementterminal.
Best Colleges. "Best Online Bachelor's in Library Science Programs." Accessed September 21, 2018. https://www.bestcolleges.com/features/top-online-library-science-programs/.
Bookjobs.com. "Major/Department Guide." Association of American Publishers, Inc. Accessed September 20, 2018. http://www.bookjobs.com/major-to-department-guide.
Bureau of Labor Statistics. "Computer and Information Technology Occupations." *Occupational Outlook Handbook*. United States Department of Labor. Last modified April 13, 2018. https://www.bls.gov/ooh/computer-and-information-technology/home.htm.
———. "Job Openings and Labor Turnover Summary." Economic News Release. United States Department of Labor. Accessed April 12, 2018. https://www.bls.gov/news.release/jolts.nr0.htm.
———. "Librarians." *Occupational Outlook Handbook*. US Department of Labor. Last modified July 2, 2018. https://www.bls.gov/ooh/education-training-and-library/librarians.htm.

———. "Library Technicians and Assistants." *Occupational Outlook Handbook*. United States Department of Labor. Last modified April 13, 2018. https://www.bls.gov/ooh/education-training-and-library/mobile/library-technicians-and-assistants.htm.

———. "Number of Jobs Held, Labor Market Activity, and Earnings Growth among the Youngest Baby Boomers: Results from a Longitudinal Survey Summary." Economic News Release. United States Department of Labor. August 24, 2017. https://www.bls.gov/news.release/nlsoy.nr0.htm.

———. "Occupational Outlook Handbook." Last modified April 13, 2018. https://www.bls.gov/ooh/.

———. "Publishing Industries (Except Internet): NAICS 511." Industries at a Glance. United States Department of Labor. Accessed October 30, 2018. https://www.bls.gov/iag/tgs/iag511.htm.

CareerBuilder. "About CareerBuilder." Accessed April 11, 2018. https://hiring.careerbuilder.com/company/overview?_ga=2.114826119.125216564.1523526407-124352660.1467671469.

Cavazos, Nicole. "How to Rehearse for a Job Interview." ZipRecruiter (blog). Accessed September 9, 2018. https://www.ziprecruiter.com/blog/how-to-rehearse-for-a-job-interview/.

Chilton. "About Us." Accessed September 7, 2018. http://www.chilton.cengage.com/home/about.

Cleveland Clinic. "Library Staff and Mission." Accessed December 7, 2018. https://portals.clevelandclinic.org/library/About-the-Library/Library-Staff-Mission.

DHI Group. "We Are Specialized!" Accessed April 12, 2018. https://www.dhigroupinc.com/home-page/default.aspx.

Drexel University. "Sample Interview Questions." Steinbright Career Development Center. Accessed December 6, 2018. https://drexel.edu/scdc/professional-pointers/interviewing/sample-interview-questions/.

Eastern Kentucky University. "Master of Arts in Education—School Media Librarian." Library Science. Accessed August 12, 2018. https://libraryscience.eku.edu/master-arts-education-emphasis-library-science#_ga=2.186398639.741576739.1534121671-631974144.1534121671.

———. "School Media Librarian P-12 Certification Program." Library Science. Accessed August 12, 2018. https://libraryscience.eku.edu/school-media-librarian-k-12-certification-program.

EBSCO Information Services. "Metadata Librarian I." Careers. Accessed October 14, 2018. https://careers.ebscoind.com/ebscoinformationservices/job/Durham-Metadata-Librarian-I-NC-27713/494445300/.

Electronic Resources and Libraries. "ER&L in a Snapshot." Accessed September 21, 2018. https://www.electroniclibrarian.org/about/erl-in-a-snapshot/.

Florida State University Libraries. "Library and Technology Jobs: Library Interview Questions." Last updated May 5, 2017. http://guides.lib.fsu.edu/c.php?g=352933&p=2383379.

Foxworth, Deloris J., and Roseann H. Polashek. "Public Library Summer Reading Registration on Google Forms." In *The Complete Guide to Using Google in Libraries: Research, User Applications and Networking*, vol. 2, edited by Carol Smallwood, 133–44. Lanham, MD: Rowman & Littlefield, 2015.

Glassdoor. "About Us." Accessed April 9, 2018. https://www.glassdoor.com/about/index_input.htm.

Hardenbrook, Joe. "Library Interview Questions." Nailing the Library Interview. *Mr. Library Dude* (blog). Accessed September 25, 2018. https://mrlibrarydude.wordpress.com/nailing-the-library-interview/library-interview-questions/.

Hernandez, Richard. "Online Job Search: The New Normal." Bureau of Labor Statistics. February 2017. https://www.bls.gov/opub/mlr/2017/beyond-bls/online-job-search-the-new-normal.htm.

House, Naomi. "About *INALJ*." *INALJ*. Accessed September 21, 2018. http://inalj.com/?page_id=10653.

———. "Volunteer at *INALJ*." *INALJ*. Accessed September 21, 2018. http://inalj.com/?page_id=47338.

———. "Write for *INALJ*." *INALJ*. Accessed September 21, 2018. http://inalj.com/?page_id=65207.

Indeed. "About Indeed." Accessed April 11, 2018. https://www.indeed.com/about.

Indiana Library Federation. "Career Center: Interview Questions." Accessed December 6, 2018. https://www.ilfonline.org/networking/.

Indiana University–Bloomington. "Libraries: Hours." Accessed September 23, 2018. https://libraries.indiana.edu/wells/hours.

Isaacs, Kim. "Is a Combination Résumé Right for You?" Advice. Monster. Accessed October 28, 2018. https://www.monster.com/career-advice/article/is-a-combination-resume-right-for-you.

Jefferson County Public Schools. "Library Media Specialist." Accessed September 21, 2018. https://www.applitrack.com/jefferson/onlineapp/default.aspx?AppliTrackPostingSearch=location:%22HITE+ELEMENTARY%22.

Kentucky Department for Libraries and Archives. "Continuing Education Events." Accessed December 7, 2018. https://kdla.ky.gov/librarians/staffdevelopment/Pages/ContinuingEducationCalendar.aspx.

———. "Kentucky State Board for the Certification of Librarians: Certification Manual 2017." Librarians: Library Staff Development: Certification Program for Kentucky Public Libraries. October 1, 2017. https://kdla.ky.gov/librarians/staffdevelopment/Documents/2017CertificationManual.pdf.

———. "Types and Requirements for Certification." Librarians: Library Staff Development: Certification Program for Kentucky Public Libraries. Last updated 2010. https://kdla.ky.gov/librarians/staffdevelopment/Documents/CertReq.pdf.

Kentucky Virtual Library. "About KYVL." Last updated November 6, 2018. https://www.kyvl.org/about.

Kodaira, Nanako. "Academic Interview Process." American Library Association, New Members Round Table. Accessed December 6, 2018. http://www.ala.org/rt/nmrt/oversightgroups/comm/resreview/process.

LAC Group. "Top Five Skills Required for Librarians." August 6, 2016. https://lac-group.com/top-five-skills-required-for-librarians-today-tomorrow/.

The Library Collective. "The Collective Annual Gathering." Accessed August 12, 2018. http://www.thelibrarycollective.org/libcol/.

The Library Corporation. "Sales Engineer." Accessed October 14, 2018. https://tlcdelivers.com/job/sales-engineer/.

Lincoln County Library System. "Careers at Lincoln County Library." Accessed October 14, 2018. https://linclib.org/careers.

Lincoln, Ruth. "Conflict in the Job Interview: How to Approach the Tricky Questions." *INALJ*. October 4, 2013, and August 29, 2014. http://inalj.com/?p=42145.

LinkedIn. "380 Masters in Library Science Jobs, Careers in Worldwide." Jobs. Accessed September 21, 2018. https://www.linkedin.com/jobs/search/?keywords=masters%20in%20library%20science&location=Worldwide&locationId=OTHERS.worldwide&start=125.

Maine State Library. "Library Job Descriptions." Accessed December 6, 2018. https://www.maine.gov/msl/libs/admin/jobdesc.shtml.

McNally, Brad. "Behavioral Interviews (And How You Can Use Them to Your Advantage)." *INALJ*. April 7, 2014. http://inalj.com/?p=67484.

Minnis, Sarah. "Skills Matrix." University of Kentucky, Lewis Honors College. Accessed November 28, 2018. http://www.uky.edu/honors/sites/www.uky.edu.honors/files/Skills%20Matrix.pdf.

Monster. "About Monster Worldwide." Accessed April 12, 2018. https://www.monster.com/about/.

———. "Should Your Résumé Be in the Past or Present Tense?" Advice. Accessed September 21, 2018. https://www.monster.com/career-advice/article/past-or-present-tense.

NASIG. "Learn about NASIG: Publications." Accessed August 18, 2018. https://nasig.wordpress.com/learn-about-nasig/publications/.

Neal, James (@jamesneal). Twitter post. December 29, 2017, 1:25 p.m. https://twitter.com/jamesneal/status/946854738435411968.

Nelson Rendón, Joanna. "Ace the Interview." *Public Libraries Online*. May 8, 2014. http://publiclibrariesonline.org/2014/05/ace-the-interview/.

New Mexico State Library. "Library Job Descriptions." Accessed December 6, 2018. http://www.nmstatelibrary.org/services-for-nm-libraries/programs-services/librarians-toolkit/library-job-descriptions.

Northern Kentucky University. "Workshop Schedules." Library Science Education Programs. Accessed August 12, 2018. https://inside.nku.edu/libraryeducation/librarycareerdevelopment/workshops.html.

OCLC. "Discover. Innovate. Collaborate. Inform. Make a Meaningful Difference at OCLC: Who We Are." Careers. Accessed September 26, 2018. https://www.oclc.org/en/careers.html.

———. "Together We Make Breakthroughs Possible." About. Accessed September 26, 2018. https://www.oclc.org/en/about.html.

ProQuest. "Databases." Accessed September 7, 2018. https://www.proquest.com/products-services/databases/.

Robert Half International. "Employers: Simplify Your Search for Top Tech Talent." Work With Us: Our Services: Technology and IT. Accessed September 20, 2018. https://www.roberthalf.com/work-with-us/our-services/technology#employers.

———. "Job Seekers: How We Help You Find an IT Job—Fast." Work With Us: Our Services: Technology and IT. Accessed September 20, 2018. https://www.roberthalf.com/work-with-us/our-services/technology#jobseekers.

———. "2019 Technology & IT Salary Guide." Accessed September 23, 2018. https://www.roberthalf.com/salary-guide/technology.

Routledge, Taylor & Francis Group. "The Serials Librarian." Accessed August 18, 2018. https://amo_hub_content.s3.amazonaws.com/Association92/files/Publications/WSER%20Nasig%20member%20rate.pdf.

San José State University, School of Information. "Behavioral Interview Questions." Accessed September 25, 2018. http://ischool.sjsu.edu/behavioral-interview-questions.

———. "Benefits to Using Placement Agencies." College of Health and Human Services. Accessed June 24, 2018. http://ischool.sjsu.edu/career-development/job-search-and-agencies/placement-agencies/benefits-using-placement-agencies.

Schwartz, Meredith. "Top Skills for Tomorrow's Librarians: Careers 2016." *Library Journal*. March 9, 2016. https://www.libraryjournal.com/?detailStory=top-skills-for-tomorrows-librarians-careers-2016.
SimplyHired. "Post Jobs Free." Accessed April 12, 2018. https://www.simplyhired.com/post-jobs-free.
Society for Human Resource Management. "Interview Questions." Accessed July 4, 2018. https://www.shrm.org/ResourcesAndTools/tools-and-samples/interview-questions/Pages/default.aspx.
Taylor & Francis Group. "*The Serials Librarian*: Aims and Scope." Accessed August 18, 2018. https://www.tandfonline.com/action/journalInformation?show=aimsScope&journalCode=wser20.
———. "*The Serials Librarian*: Instructions for Authors." Accessed August 18, 2018. https://www.tandfonline.com/action/authorSubmission?journalCode=wser20&page=instructions.
———. "*The Serials Librarian*: Journal Information." Accessed August 19, 2018. https://www.tandfonline.com/action/journalInformation?show=aimScope&journalCode=wser20.
TechSoup Global. "Writing Guidelines for the Blog." Accessed September 21, 2018. https://www.techsoup.org/writing-guidelines-for-blog.
Triffin, Molly. "Interview Etiquette: Is the Handwritten Thank You Note Outdated?" June 9, 2014. https://www.forbes.com/sites/learnvest/2014/06/09/interview-etiquette-is-the-handwritten-thank-you-note-outdated/#52dd217314c9.
University of Illinois. "Job Details." Human Resources. Accessed October 14, 2018. https://jobs.illinois.edu/faculty-positions/job-details?jobID=103397&job=school-of-information-sciences-senior-lecturer-103397.
University of Illinois, College of Law Library. "LIS 530 GLE: Legal Resources: The Interview Process." Last updated December 4, 2018. https://libguides.law.illinois.edu/c.php?g=494760&p=3685748 .
University of Illinois, Graduate College. "Getting Ready to Negotiate." Career Development. Accessed July 26, 2018. https://grad.illinois.edu/careers/negot-prep.
University of Kentucky. "Data Management Specialist Sr." Jobs. Accessed September 16, 2018. https://ukjobs.uky.edu/posting/199582.
———. "Equivalencies." Human Resources. Accessed December 6, 2018. http://www.uky.edu/hr/employment/working-uk/equivalencies.
University of North Carolina, University Library. "Sample Interview Questions." October 2014. "https://library.unc.edu/wp-content/uploads/2014/10/interview-questions.pdf.

University of South Carolina. "Event Coordinator." Jobs. Accessed September 21, 2018. https://uscjobs.sc.edu/postings/40628.

University of Southern California, Marshall School of Business. "Skills Today's Library Science Students Need for Career Success." *MMLIS Blog.* Accessed September 21, 2018. https://librarysciencedegree.usc.edu/blog/skills-todays-library-science-students-need-for-career-success/.

University of Washington, Information School. "Job Interviews: Frequently Asked Interview Questions." Advising and Support. Accessed December 6, 2018. https://ischool.uw.edu/advising-support/career-services/interviews.

———. "Sample Interview Questions: LIS Specific and Generic." Google Doc. Accessed December 6, 2018. https://docs.google.com/file/d/1g8fEGe0KoVrKwODXyvQButA7D4qRdG7oURhUxvou0lWtzG9QU7eFzjrA7xML/edit?hl=en&pli=1.

Vasiliver-Shamis, Gaia. "6 Mistakes to Avoid When Negotiating Your Job Offer." *Inside Higher Ed.* April 23, 2018. https://www.insidehighered.com/advice/2018/04/23/how-negotiate-job-offer-effectively-opinion.

Vinjamuri, David. "The Case for Libraries." *Publishers Weekly.* April 3, 2015. https://www.publishersweekly.com/pw/by-topic/industry-news/libraries/article/66106-the-case-for-libraries.html.

Weak, Emily. "*Hiring Librarians*' Library Interview Question 'Database.'" *Hiring Librarians* (blog). Accessed September 25, 2018. http://tinyurl.com/InterviewQuestionsRepository.

———. Search results for "Interview Questions Repository." *Hiring Librarians* (blog). Accessed December 6, 2018. https://hiringlibrarians.com/?s=Interview+Questions+Repository.

World Economic Forum. "The Future of Jobs: Employment, Skills and Workforce Strategy for the Fourth Industrial Revolution." January 2016. http://www3.weforum.org/docs/WEF_Future_of_Jobs.pdf.

Young Adult Library Services Association. "YALSA's 2018 Young Adult Services Symposium." Accessed December 7, 2018. http://www.ala.org/yalsa/yasymposium.

Zaayer Kaufman, Caroline. "Job Interview Thank You: Is It Better to Send a Letter or Email?" Advice. Monster. Accessed October 21, 2018. https://www.monster.com/career-advice/article/interview-thank-you-email-letter.

ZipRecruiter. "About." Accessed April 12, 2018. https://www.ziprecruiter.com/about.

Index

AALL. *See* American Association of Law Libraries
AASL. *See* American Association of School Librarians
accepting the job, 29, 45, 105, 117, 126–27, 131–35
ACRL. *See* Association of College and Research Libraries
action verbs, 56–57, 63–64
administration, *4*, 5
administrative support staff, 3, 9, 10
AIM, 24, 226–28
ALA. *See* American Library Association
The Annoyed Librarian, 157
American Association of Law Libraries, 142, 147, 149, 169
American Association of School Librarians, 146, 155, 169
American Library Association, 25, 32, 34, 54, 122, 143, 144, 145, 146, 151, 159, 169
applicant pool, 54, 88
applicant screening, 26, 137
 software, 57–58

application, 11, 29, 44–45, 48, 49, 53, 57–59, 62, 72, 74–77, 79, 80–*82*, 134, 137–38
application materials, 39, 48–53, 55, 57–58, 60–61, 72, 75, 77, 79, 81, 90, 94–95, 99, 119, 128, 135, 137–38, 156
application process, 24, 26, 29, 44, 49, 50, 56–58, 72, 76, 77, 85, 117, 137
ASIS&T. *See* Association of Information Science and Technology
ask questions, 105–8, 110–11, 127, 138
association, 5, 15, 28, 32, 34, 70–71, 94–95, 97, *101*,147–51, 157, 169. *See also* library association, professional association
Association of College and Research Libraries, 144, 159, 170
Association of Information Science and Technology, 16, 25, 28, 55, 170

benefits, 31, 105, 108, 122–24, 126–28, *130*, 133, 142, 148

blogging, 155–56. *See also* social media: blog
Bureau of Labor Statistics, 1, 23, 122, 141. *See also* Occupational Outlook Handbook, US Department of Labor

certificate, 9, 142–43, 146, 161
certification, 9, 68, 141–49, 151, 169
College and Research Libraries News, 157
conferences, 39, 147, 149–54, 162
connections, 28–29, 33, 37–39, 73, 133–34. *See also* network, networking
continuing education, 144, 147–49, 151
cover letter, 51–53, 55, 58–61, 71–75, 79–*82*, 95, 162, 179, 180
curriculum vitae, 52, 55, 58–61, 69–76, 79–81, 135, 154, 158, 162, 173, 175–76, 177
CV. *See* curriculum vitae

declining, 117, 135–36
degree, 1, *2*, 3, 5, 9–10, 14–15, 23, 26, 30, 38, 45, 54, 65, 142–47, 161;
 associate's, *2*, 9, 54, 143;
 bachelor's, *2*, 9, 54, 143;
 doctorate, 54 (*see also* PhD);
 master's, 3, 5, 14–15, 43, 54–55, 143–46;
 PhD, 69, 144. *See also* education

Eastern Kentucky University, 146
e-tutorials, 147–50
education, 1–*2*, 5–6, 8–10, 13–14, 18, 37, 41, 43–44, 56, 59, 61–62, 65–70, 74, 76, 95, 97, 99, 104, 125, 144, 147;
 area of study, 54–55. *See also* degree
employment, 1–3, 10–14, 16, 24, 28–33, 37–38, 40, 43, 54, 56, 58, 61–63, 67–68, 70–71, 73, 76–77, 79, 85, 131–32, 134–37, 145, 147
evaluate, 54, 56, 60, 99, 103, 109, 121–22
experience, 52–59, 61–64, 66–71, 74, 76, 88, 88, 93, 95, 97–99, 104–5, 118, 128, 133, 138, 145, 152, 156, 160

Florida State University Libraries, 96

hiring, 13, 14, 24, 30, 35–36, 38–39, 44–45, 55, 58–60, 72–74, 77, 86–87, 89–91, 95–96, 106, 110, 120, 137
hiring process, 31, 44–45, 60, 86, 90, 107

INALJ, 34–35, 97, 155–56
I need a library job. *See* INALJ
interview, 29, 31, 45, 52, 72–75, 79, 81–*82*, 85–100, 103–12, 117–21, 128, 129, 134, 135, 137, 138, 157
 academic interview, 97, 110;
 academic library interview, 93 (*see also* academic interview);
 combination interview, 92;
 computer-mediated interview, 87–89, 112;
 face-to-face interview, 86–87, 89–90, 109, 112;
 group interview, 91–92;
 interview format, 90;
 interview methods, 85;

interview purpose, 85;
one-on-one interview, 90–91;
panel interview, 91–93;
presentation interview, 92–93;
technology-assisted interview, 86–89, 94 (*see also* computer-mediated interview)
interview questions, 29, 96–100, 103, 105, 138;
behavioral, 29, 96, 97, 99, 104;
general, 98;
hypothetical, 97;
situational, 97–99;
theoretical, 97

job announcement, 24, 26, 29, 32, 34, 43. *See also* job description
job application, 75–76. *See also* application
job board, 23–26, 29–31, 36, 41, 44, 78–80, 169
job description, 42, 49–57, 62, 66 67, 70, 77–81, 94–95, 99, 107, 121;
job duties, 50, 52–53, 107, 121, 127–28, 131
minimum requirements, 53–55, 58, 137 (*see also* minimum qualifications);
minimum qualifications, 50, 53–54, 58 (*see also* minimum requirements);
position title, 50–51, 80–*82*;
qualitative requirements, 55;
quantitative requirements, 55–56.
See also job announcement
job-hunting, 23, 77, 93
job search, 1, 3, 11, 14, 17, 23–24, 26–28, 30, 32–36, 38–39, 41, 44–45, 59, 78, 80, 96, 137–38

Kentucky Department for Libraries and Archives, 16, 151
Kentucky Virtual Library, 16
KYVL. *See* Kentucky Virtual Library

LAC Group, 26–27, 42
LibGig, 24, 26, 28, 35
librarian, 1–9, 15, 26, 34–38, 41–42, 54–55, 58, 61, 66, 70–72, 92–93, 95–96, 102, 121, 142–46, 150–51, 154–56, 158–60. *See also* professional staff
librarianship, 11–*12*, 71, 142
librarian technician, 2–3, 9–10, 143. *See also* library assistant
library assistant, 2–3, 9–10, 121. *See also* librarian technician
library association, 15, 34, 95, 97, *101*, 145, 148, 157. *See also* association, professional association
Library Career People, 35, 156
Library Collective, 150
library certification, 144
Library Information Technology Association, 52, 160–61
Library Journal, 42, 122, 157
library vendors, 11–*12*, 16, 92, 95, 148
lifelong learning, 142. *See also* professional development
LISTSERV, 13–14, 23, 32, 148, 152, 160–61, 169
LITA. *See* Library Information Technology Association
location, 3, 6, 24–26, 28–30, 33–34, 37, 55, 53, 56, 62, 67–68, 70, 78, 87, 94, 121–22, 124–25, 127–28, *130*, 135
log, *82*, 138

manager, 2–6, 11, 50–52, 72, 74, 77, 90, 96, 131
Mr. Library Dude, 36, 97

negotiation, 105, 117, 126–31, 135; counter offer, 129, 131, 135; leverage, 128–29
network, 26, 28, 33, 37–39, 41, 147, 149, 150. *See also* connections, networking
networking, 33, 39–40, 149. *See also* connections, network
New Mexico State Library, 50, 55
NH Library Jobline, 35
nonessential duties, 50, 52
Northern Kentucky University, 149
notice, 126, *130*–32, 137–38

obligations, 45
occupation, 16, 17
Occupational Outlook Handbook, 95, 122. *See also* Bureau of Labor Statistics, US Department of Labor
occupational path, 16–17, 25, 28
offer, 81–*82*, 108, 117, 121–23, 126–27, 129–31, 135–37
online tools, 23, 37

paraprofessional library staff, 2–3, 6, 9, 142–44
PLA. *See* Public Library Association
placement agencies, 24, 26, 28, 42
planning, 96, 98–*101*, 103–8, 111
position description, 72
position title, 50–51, 80–*82*
practice, 94, 108–9, 129
preparation, 92, 96, 98, 105, 109–10
preparing, 85, 93, 98

professional association, 13, 15–16, 24–25, 29, 32, 39, 71, 95, 108, 147–49, 151, 160, 169. *See also* association, library association
professional development, 16, 38, 71, *101*, 108, 141–42, 147–50, 157, 162, 169
professional resources, 147
professional staff, 3, *4*. *See also* librarian
proposals, 51, 57, 70, 151–54, 158–59, 161
publication, 45, 70, 107, 152, 155, 158–62
Public Library Association, 97, 171
publisher, 11–*12*, 160–61
publishing, 155, 157–59
publishing industry, 11, *12*
reference, 26, 29, 38–39, 76–77, 79, 131, 134

reference interview, 2, 8
rejection, 117, 136–38, 154
research, 92, 94–96, 106, 127–28, 151, 157, 161
résumé, 28, 30, 36, 51–53, 55, 58–69, 71–76, 79–*82*, 95, 119, 135, 154, 158, 162; chronological resume, 62–64, 66, 68; combination resume, 62, 68–69; functional resume, 62, 66–68; professional profile, 68

salary, 30–31, 36, 44, 56–57, 95, 105, 108, 121–24, 126–27, 129–31, 136, 142
San Jose State University, 26, 96
school media specialist, 3–5, 7
search parameters, 41, 44

search terminology, 41, 44
self-publish, 158, 161
self-reflection, 117–19, 138
SJSU. *See* San Jose State University
skills, 1, 5, 8, 10–*12*, 14–15, 28, 30, 33, 36, 41–43, 57–62, 64, 66–68, 72–74, 76, 88–89, 92–93, 95, 97–100, 104–5, 108, 133, 138, 142–43, 152, 154, 156
skills matrix, 100, 102, 108
social media, 23, 32, 38, 40, 50, 76, 135, 147, 148, 152, 157, 160, 161;
 blog, 32, 35, 36, 97, 155–58, 160–61;
 LinkedIn, 28–29, 32–35, 38, 41, 43, 61, 76;
 Pinterest, 78;
 Twitter, 32, 34, 35, 61
STAR method, 96, 97, 99, 100, 103–04, 109, 111;
 action, 96, 99–102;
 result, 96, 100–04;
 situation, 96, 99–104;
 task, 96, 99–104
supervisor, 29, 33, 38–39, 50, 53, 89–90, 100, 102, 105, 108, 118, 121, 131–34
supervisory, 6, 50, 53, 74, 102, 145
support staff, 10, 16, 26, 143, 145. *See also* paraprofessional library staff

technical services, *4*–8, 13, 143, 170
thank you notes, 117, 119–20
types of organization:
 affiliated, 9, 13, 15, 94–95;
 consortium, 5, 13, 15–16, 95;
 cooperative, 13, 15–16, 95;
 parent, 9, 11, 13, 14

UK. *See* University of Kentucky
University of Illinois, 55, 93, 127
University of Kentucky, 56, 58, 100, 102, 106, 146
University of Southern California, 42
US Department of Labor, 23. *See also* Bureau of Labor Statistics, Occupational Outlook Handbook

volunteer, 63–64, 68

webinars, 147–50
work hours, 56, 121, 125, 130, 146
working conditions, 50, 53, 95, 122, 124
writing, 151, 153, 155–57

YALSA. *See* Young Adult Library Service Association
Young Adult Library Service Association, 108, 151, 154, 171

About the Author

Deloris Jackson Foxworth is an academic advisor in the College of Communication and Information at the University of Kentucky, where she also teaches part-time in their School of Information Science. She has taught classes on information literacy, personal knowledge management, and information communication–technology industries and careers.

Before joining UK's School of Information Science faculty in 2014, she was technology manager at the Scott County Public Library in Georgetown, Kentucky. Her first library position was as a student worker at Bosworth Memorial Library at the Lexington Theological Seminary.

In 2018 she earned a graduate certificate in career services from Western Kentucky University, where she already held an MA in communication. She also holds an MS in library and information science from UK.

www.ingramcontent.com/pod-product-compliance
Lightning Source LLC
Chambersburg PA
CBHW031551300426
44111CB00006BA/260